Super Easy and Delicious

LUNCHES FOR KIDS

Quarto.com

© 2024 Quarto Publishing Group USA Inc.
Text © 2014 Laura Fuentes

First Published in 2024 by New Shoe Press, an imprint of The Quarto Group,
100 Cummings Center, Suite 265-D, Beverly, MA 01915, USA.
T (978) 282-9590 F (978) 283-2742

Essential, In-Demand Topics, Four-Color Design, Affordable Price
New Shoe Press publishes affordable, beautifully designed books covering evergreen, in-demand subjects. With a goal to inform and inspire readers' everyday hobbies, from cooking and gardening to wellness and health to art and crafts, New Shoe titles offer the ultimate library of purposeful, how-to guidance aimed at meeting the unique needs of each reader. Reimagined and redesigned from Quarto's best-selling backlist, New Shoe books provide practical knowledge and opportunities for all DIY enthusiasts to enrich and enjoy their lives.

Visit Quarto.com/New-Shoe-Press for a complete listing of the New Shoe Press books.

New Shoe Press titles are also available at discount for retail, wholesale, promotional, and bulk purchase. For details, contact the Special Sales Manager by email at specialsales@quarto.com or by mail at The Quarto Group, Attn: Special Sales Manager, 100 Cummings Center, Suite 265-D, Beverly, MA 01915, USA.

10 9 8 7 6 5 4 3 2 1

ISBN: 978-0-7603-9074-0
eISBN: 978-0-7603-9075-7

The content in this book was previously published in *The Best Homemade Kids' Lunches on the Planet* (Fair Winds Press 2014) by Laura Fuentes.

Library of Congress Cataloging-in-Publication Data available

Photography: Alison Bickel Photography

Printed in China

Super Easy and Delicious
LUNCHES FOR KIDS

Deliciously Nutritious Meal Ideas Your Kids Will Love

LAURA FUENTES

NEW SHOE PRESS

Contents

Introduction

I used to stare at the refrigerator every morning, waiting for food to talk to me and say, "Pick me! Pack me inside the lunchbox!" Unfortunately, the longer I stared, the longer the food stayed silent.

At the grocery store, I swear those brightly colored boxes holding premade lunches would actually speak to my daughter, saying "I am fun! You'll love me for lunch! And don't tell your mom, but I have really bad ingredients!"

I remember the first week of my daughter's two-day-a-week preschool. I was so excited to make perfect little lunches with fresh fruits and neatly stacked veggies. I also remember the disappointment I felt three weeks later when I didn't know what else to pack for her. The truth: I was stumped for ideas.

Adding to my lack of ideas were food allergies to take into consideration. After extensive food journaling, I was able to determine that my little girl was allergic to disodium phosphates and chemical nitrates. Fortunately, the easiest way to avoid these is to purchase real foods, including natural and organic meats, and become food label savvy.

But at that point in my life, I had a two- month-old at home, I was sleep-deprived, and time was of the essence. While I could cook just about anything, I wasn't very organized in the kitchen (yet), so we were spending more money than I would have liked for healthy convenience foods—and I was becoming a short-order cook.

By the time my oldest kids were two and three years old, they were both attending preschool a few days a week. Because they didn't complain about the same lunches being served often, I continued to do the same rotation of three lunches for them. Yet, inside, I knew I could and should do better.

One day, I ran out of sandwich bread, and I decided to use leftover pancakes from breakfast night instead. That lunch was immediately a hit with my daughter, and her excitement and request for more fun lunches was all the motivation I needed to do better.

From that day forward, and for the past four years, I've been giving kid-appeal to real foods, making my own versions of those store-bought lunches that kids like so much with fresh ingredients, and helping thousands feed their children better school lunches through MOMables.com.

Along the way, I've learned how to pack foods so that they don't become soggy inside the lunchbox, tested nearly every lunch container out there, and developed hundreds of recipes.

I attribute much of my creativity to my two oldest kids being very picky eaters. They often refuse to try new foods and continue to be a challenge in the kitchen. Most of the recipes I develop are my attempts at sneaking more nutrition into foods my oldest two will actually eat. My youngest, on the other hand, is the complete opposite. He was born six months after I launched MOMables and, since then, has volunteered much of his time to taste-testing many of my recipes. Thankfully, he is nearly always willing to try something new!

This book has many of my family's favorite recipes and kitchen shortcuts, so you can make lunches quickly and healthfully. I also share my tips on how to freeze, store, and repurpose leftovers, so that less food is wasted and you can stretch your grocery budget even further.

Not only that, but you'll also be able to use the recipes whether you have kids in kindergarten or high school, because the recipes in this book can

be adjusted for portion size. And, if you really want to go all out in lunch packing, you can be like my family and use these recipes for adults too. They're made for everyone!

Packing a healthy school lunch should not be complicated. All you need are some great recipes, fresh ingredients, and the willingness to try a few new things. I hope that in the following pages, you find inspiration to make lunchtime a success!

CHAPTER ONE

Get Out the Door: Breakfasts to Go

My kids are turtle slow in the morning, so by the time they sit down for breakfast it's nearly always time to go! Growing tired of half-eaten bagels and soggy pancakes, one day, I decided to fill an empty lunch container with their breakfast. If the kids were able to finish their breakfast at the table, great. If not, they could easily take it to-go! The recipes included in this section are portable, delicious, and kid-approved. They are also the building blocks of some of our fun breakfast lunches.

Perfect Pancakes

I have my Auntie Colleen to thank for this recipe. Once, while staying at her house, she made these beautiful pancakes with fresh blueberries from her farmers' market. They were fluffy, not overly sweet, and easy to make—simply amazing! Of course, I asked her for the recipe, and 15 years later, I am still making these at least once a week.

1½ cups (200 g) all-purpose flour

3½ teaspoons (16 g) baking powder

½ teaspoon salt

1 tablespoon (13 g) sugar

1¼ cups (294 ml) milk

1 egg

3 tablespoons (42 g) butter, melted (optional), plus more for serving

Maple syrup, for serving

—
YIELD: 10 pancakes

In a large bowl, sift together the flour, baking powder, salt, and sugar. Make a well (or volcano, as my son calls it) in the middle, and pour in the milk, egg, and melted butter, if using; mix with a fork or whisk until smooth.

Heat a griddle or large pan over medium-high heat (I set my griddle at 375°F [190°C]).

Pour or scoop ¼ cup (125 g) of batter for each pancake. Wait until bubbles form on the top to flip. Brown on the other side and serve with butter and maple syrup.

KITCHEN NOTES

To substitute or make with:

100 PERCENT WHOLE WHEAT FLOUR: Add an additional teaspoon of baking powder and an additional tablespoon (15 ml) of milk.

50 PERCENT WHOLE WHEAT FLOUR (HALF ALL-PURPOSE, HALF WHOLE WHEAT): Add ½ teaspoon baking powder.

GLUTEN-FREE FLOUR MIX: Use a 1:1 substitution ratio for the flour. For optimal results, I suggest King Arthur Flour Gluten Free All-Purpose Mix

FLAX: Add ¼ cup (28 g) ground flax and remove ¼ cup (31 g) flour; add ½ teaspoon baking powder.

You can also add 1 medium mashed banana or up to 1 cup (155 g) blueberries or nuts to the original recipe or one of the variations above.

I also love to double or triple this recipe and substitute the pancakes for bread in school lunches. Store the extra batches in the freezer so you can grab them whenever needed.

Kitchen Sink Muffins

My favorite kinds of recipes are those that are flexible and will yield delicious results. Recipes that, on any given day, I can make work with what I might have in my pantry. These muffins are just that kind of recipe. When you mix and match any of the add-ins, even your pickiest eater is sure to find a combination that they will love.

FOR MUFFINS:

2 cups (250 g) whole wheat pastry flour

2 tablespoons (14 g) ground flax meal

2 teaspoons (9 g) baking powder

1 teaspoon baking soda

⅓ cup (67 g) granulated sugar

1 cup (245 g) unsweetened applesauce

2 tablespoons (28 g) melted butter

⅓ cup (78 ml) milk

FOR ADD-INS:

1 cup (155 g) fresh or frozen fruit, such as blueberries, thawed

½ cup (55 g) pecans, walnuts, or almonds, chopped

⅔ cup (97 g) dried fruit, such as raisins

1 teaspoon (3 g) ground cinnamon

1 cup (175 g) semi-sweet chocolate chips

—
YIELD: 12 muffins

Preheat the oven to 400°F (200°C) and line a standard-size muffin pan with liners.

In a large mixing bowl, combine the dry ingredients. Add in the applesauce, melted butter, and milk, and stir until thoroughly combined, creating a smooth, stiff batter.

Gently fold in the add-ins, if using, and then divide the batter equally, spooning it into the muffin cups.

Bake the muffins for 15 to 20 minutes, or until the tops are golden. Transfer to a cooling rack. Serve warm or at room temperature. Store the remaining muffins in an airtight container.

LAURA'S TIP

You can freeze muffins after they are baked and cooled for future grab-and-go breakfasts. To rewarm, heat the muffin for 10 to 15 seconds in the microwave.

Eggs-to-Go

There is no such thing as "no time for breakfast" when you have a pan of these ready to go in your fridge!

12 eggs

¾ cup (175 ml) milk

Veggies (green and red bell peppers, onions, mushrooms, tomatoes, etc.), chopped

Meat (diced ham, turkey sausage, bacon, etc.)

Shredded Cheddar cheese (for topping)

Preheat the oven to 375°F (190°C) and grease or spray a standard 12-cup muffin tin.

In a large bowl, whisk the eggs and milk. Pour the egg mixture evenly into the greased wells until each well is about half full. Add in the veggies, and top with the meat and cheese.

Top off each well with the additional egg mixture (being careful to leave a little room at the top), and bake for 18 to 20 minutes.

Remove from the oven, pop them out of each well, and serve. Allow extras to cool before storing in the refrigerator.

—
YIELD: 12 servings

Breakfast Burrito >

No more frozen breakfast burritos with mystery ingredients, or a quick trip to the drive-through. This is the perfect make-ahead recipe that your entire family will love!

1 tablespoon (16 g) Homemade Salsa (page 114)

1 tablespoon (15 g) sour cream

One 8-inch (20 cm) tortilla

1 large egg, scrambled

2 tablespoons (15 g) shredded cheese

1 slice (7 g) bacon, cooked and crumbled

In a small bowl, the mix salsa and sour cream.

Lay the tortilla on a cutting board, and spread the salsa mixture evenly on the middle third. Lay the egg, cheese, and bacon on top. Fold the sides in, and then roll into a burrito.

For the lunchbox: Wrap in parchment paper and a thin layer of foil to retain the heat (optional). If you must have these warm, cut them in half and insert face up inside a thermos.

—
YIELD: 1 serving

KITCHEN NOTE

Get a pack (or two) of flour tortillas and make extra breakfast burritos. Line a baking sheet with parchment paper, lay the burritos flat 1 inch (2.5 cm) apart and flash freeze. Transfer the frozen burritos into a freezer ziplock bag. To warm, microwave for 30 seconds to 1 minute and enjoy. Store in the freezer up to 2 months.

Breakfast Cookies

"If it looks like a cookie and tastes like a cookie, then it must be a cookie!" said Cookie Monster on Sesame Street. It is—sort of. Little do my kids know that these "cookies" have protein, fiber, vitamins, minerals, and omega 3s.

1 large banana, mashed

½ cup (130 g) peanut butter

½ cup (170 g) honey

2 teaspoons (10 ml) vanilla extract

1 cup (80 g) old-fashioned oats

¼ cup (31 g) whole wheat flour

¼ cup (28 g) ground flaxseed

¼ cup (32 g) powdered milk or vanilla protein

2 teaspoons (5 g) ground cinnamon

½ teaspoon baking soda

¾ cup (110 g) add-ins: raisins, chocolate chips, and/or dried fruit

—

YIELD: 12 cookies

Preheat the oven to 350°F (180°C) and line two cookie sheets with parchment paper.

In the bowl of your stand mixer, or a large bowl, mix the banana, peanut butter, honey, and vanilla.

In a small bowl, combine the oats, flour, flax, powdered milk, cinnamon, and baking soda.

Slowly add the dry mixture to the wet ingredients, mixing until everything is combined evenly. Fold in your add-ins, up to ¾ cup (110 g).

Using a ¼ cup (60 g) measuring cup or scoop, drop dough scoops 3 inches (7.5 cm) apart onto your lined baking sheets. Using your hands, flatten your dough scoops to about ½-inch (1.25 cm) tall. This will ensure even baking.

Bake the cookies for 15 minutes, or until lightly browned. Allow the cookies to cool for 5 minutes on the baking sheet before transferring to a wire rack to cool completely.

Store in an airtight container or resealable plastic bag for up to 3 days or freeze for up to 2 months; thaw before serving.

French Toast Stix

Breakfast for dinner is my kids' favorite, so why not serve breakfast for lunch? You'll rock their lunchbox with these delicious sticks of cinnamon goodness! You can make extras and store in the freezer for a quick breakfast too.

2 eggs

¼ cup (60 ml) milk

½ teaspoon vanilla extract

4 slices cinnamon raisin bread

Butter or butter spray for cooking

2 tablespoons (30 ml) maple syrup, for dipping

—
YIELD: 2 servings

In a shallow bowl or baking dish, whisk together the eggs, milk, and vanilla. Add the bread slices and let soak, turning once or twice, until all of the egg mixture has been absorbed (about 3 minutes).

Heat a large nonstick skillet or griddle over medium heat, and spread or spray the butter evenly over the pan bottom.

Add the soaked bread slices side by side. Cook until the bottoms are golden, about 2 minutes. Carefully flip them over. Cook until the second side is also golden and the centers puff slightly, about 2 more minutes.

Cut into strips for dipping, and serve with a side of maple syrup stored in a small container with a lid.

KITCHEN NOTE

Make these the night before, and warm them in the morning before packing for school.

Cinnamon Roll Overnight Oatmeal

My husband calls oatmeal a "stick to your belly" breakfast. It's filling, hearty, and budget-friendly. This version cooks itself while your family sleeps, and in the morning, the house smells amazing!

1 cup (80 g) steel-cut oats

4 cups (950 ml) water

½ cup (120 ml) milk

¼ cup (60 g) packed brown sugar

½ teaspoon vanilla extract

1 teaspoon cinnamon

Maple syrup, for serving

Milk, for serving

—
YIELD: 3 servings

Add all ingredients (except maple syrup and milk) into a small crockpot. Cook on low for 6 hours.

Serve with the maple syrup and milk.

LAURA'S TIP

Double or triple this batch, and keep the leftovers in your fridge for a quick and easy breakfast during the busy week ahead!

Chocolate Chip Freezer Scones

I became addicted to these scones after trying a recipe from the Culinary Institute of America. I use their basic recipe as a guide, adjusting it to suit my kids' taste preferences—adding chocolate, of course!

3 cups (375 g) all-purpose flour

½ cup (100 g) plus
3 tablespoons (40 g) sugar,
divided

2 tablespoons (28 g)
baking powder

½ teaspoon salt

½ cup (88 g) chocolate chips

2 cups (475 ml) heavy cream
or half and half

2 tablespoons (30 ml) milk

—

YIELD: 12 scones

Line a baking sheet with parchment paper.

Sift the flour into a mixing bowl, then add ½ cup (100 g) sugar, baking powder, salt, and chocolate chips.

Make a well in the center of the flour mixture (or a volcano, as my son likes to call it). Add the cream to the well, and mix with a wooden spoon, or using your hands, until the batter is evenly moistened. The dough will be a bit sticky.

Using your hands, make twelve 2-inch (5 cm) scones and place them onto the baking sheet. If the dough sticks to your hands, rub a little flour on them. Place the baking sheet in the freezer for about 2 hours, until the dough is frozen, or overnight to prevent them from "melting" when they are baked.

Preheat the oven to 350°F (180°C). Remove the baking sheet from the freezer and let the scones thaw for about 5 minutes. If you are baking all 12 scones, you will need to line a second cookie sheet and separate, because they will expand while baking. Otherwise, place the ones you don't need inside a freezer bag, and put them back in the freezer for another day.

Brush the scones with the milk and sprinkle with the additional 3 tablespoons (40 g) of reserved sugar.

Bake the scones until golden brown, about 30 to 40 minutes. Allow to cool on the baking sheet for a few minutes, then transfer to a wire rack to continue cooling.

Enjoy the same day they are made, or freeze for up to 4 weeks.

Glazed Cake Donut Muffins

What do you get when you want to satisfy your kid's donut craving, don't own a donut pan, and want a healthier version? These Glazed Cake Donut Muffins of course! Don't let the word "donut" fool you; these are okay to have for breakfast—on occasion.

FOR MUFFINS:

¼ cup (56 g) butter, softened

½ cup (100 g) evaporated cane sugar

⅓ cup (50 g) brown sugar

2 large eggs

¼ cup (61 g) applesauce

2 teaspoons (10 ml) vanilla extract

1½ teaspoons baking powder

¼ teaspoon baking soda

1 teaspoon ground cinnamon

¾ teaspoon salt

2⅔ cups (320 g) whole wheat pastry flour (or all-purpose flour)

1 cup (235 ml) milk

FOR GLAZE:

¼ cup (60 ml) milk

1 teaspoon vanilla extract

2 cups (240 g) confectioners' sugar

—

YIELD: 12 large muffins or 18 cupcake-size muffins

Preheat the oven to 400°F (200°C) and lightly grease a large or standard muffin pan, or line with cups.

To make the muffins: In the bowl of your stand mixer, or a medium-size bowl, cream together the butter and sugars until smooth. Add the eggs, applesauce, and vanilla, mixing to combine. Add the baking powder, baking soda, cinnamon, and salt, mixing on low to combine.

Slowly add the flour into the mixture in three additions, adding alternately with the milk (beginning and ending with the flour), until everything is thoroughly combined.

Spoon the thick batter evenly into the prepared pan, filling the cups nearly full.

Bake the muffins for 17 to 20 minutes, or until the muffins are a pale golden brown and a toothpick inserted in the center comes out clean. Cool on a wire rack.

To make the glaze: In a medium bowl, combine all the ingredients and stir until smooth.

Dip the top of the muffins into the glaze after they have cooled for several minutes. Serve warm, or cool on a rack and place in an airtight container. Store for a day or so at room temperature.

Lunchbox Granola

Once you learn how to make your own granola, you'll never buy store-bought again. It's great for breakfast, as a snack, or in the lunchbox.

6 cups (480 g) old-fashioned oats

1½ cups (218 g) nuts (slivered almonds, pumpkin seeds, walnuts, etc.)

1 cup (80 g) shredded sweet coconut

½ cup (73 g) whole flaxseeds

1½ cups (218 g) raisins, cranberries, or dried fruit

½ cup (120 ml) plus 2 tablespoons (30 ml) maple syrup

½ cup (75 g) brown sugar

½ cup (120 ml) coconut oil (melted), butter (melted), or vegetable oil

¾ teaspoon salt

—
YIELD: About 8 cups

Preheat the oven to 250°F (120°C).

In a large bowl, combine the dry ingredients.

In a separate bowl, combine the maple syrup, brown sugar, oil, and salt.

Add the wet ingredients to the dry and mix well (using your hands if needed), until all is evenly coated.

Divide the granola mixture onto 2 sheet pans. Cook for 50 minutes, stirring every 15 to 20 minutes, to achieve an even color

Whole Wheat Waffles

Dust off your waffle maker because your kids are going to love this wholesome breakfast staple.

½ cup (120 ml) warm water

3 tablespoons (21 g) ground flaxseed

6 tablespoons (90 g) butter, melted

1½ cups (355 ml) milk

1¾ cups (210 g) whole wheat pastry flour (all-purpose flour may be substituted)

1 tablespoon (14 g) baking powder

1 tablespoon (13 g) granulated sugar (optional)

Pinch of salt

—
YIELD: 4 to 6 waffles—sizes vary by waffle maker

Preheat your waffle maker.

In a medium bowl, mix the water and flaxseed. Let it rest for a few minutes, or until it has become thick in consistency. Add the butter and milk, and mix to combine.

In a large bowl, combine the dry ingredients. Make a well in the center, and pour in the milk mixture. Stir until just combined, because over-stirred batter can make for tough, rubbery waffles. A few lumps are okay.

Spoon a scoopful of batter onto each waffle grid. Spread the batter to within ¼ inch of the edge of the grids. Close the lid and bake until the waffle is golden brown

CHAPTER TWO

Fill the Box: Sandwiches and More

I like to think of sandwiches as the main course of any lunchbox. Yet, long gone are the days when I packed a plain ham and cheese, or a peanut butter and jelly, more than once a week. The sandwiches, wraps, and pinwheels in this book incorporate dinner leftovers, easy-to-find ingredients, and kid-friendly combinations. I promise: After you try these recipes, your kids will never think of a sandwich as a boring lunch option ever again.

Avocado Bacon Melt

When my son wouldn't try avocado, I was crushed. He said he didn't like the "cold and slimy green thing." Short of bribing him with a sweet treat, I decided to grill it, add bacon and cheese, and give it another try. He loved it. Kids—they are funny like that.

¼ avocado, mashed

2 slices (15 g) bacon, cooked and finely chopped

2 slices whole-grain bread

Olive oil, for grilling

2 slices (40 g) provolone cheese

—
YIELD: 1 serving

In a small bowl, combine the avocado and bacon.

Lay the bread slices on a cutting board. Butter or brush the outside of the bread slices with the oil. Flip them over.

Top one bread slice with provolone cheese, then place the bacon-avocado mixture on top. Top with the remaining cheese and bread slice.

Grill the sandwich on a preheated panini grill, or in a skillet over medium heat, for 3 to 4 minutes until golden brown and the cheese is melted (if using a skillet, flip halfway through).

Grilled Taco Sandwich

I always seem to have leftover taco meat from Taco Tuesdays at my house. I couldn't think of a better way to repurpose it than this, and it has become a kid favorite.

Butter, for grilling

2 slices whole-grain bread

2 slices (40 g) Cheddar cheese

2 tablespoons (25 g) cooked ground beef

1 tablespoon (6 g) black olives, sliced

¼ cup (65 g) Homemade Salsa, for dipping (page 114)

—
YIELD: 1 serving

Butter one side of both bread slices, then flip over onto a cutting board. Place cheese on top of both bread slices, top one slice with ground beef and olives, and close the sandwich.

Place the sandwich in a skillet over medium heat. Grill for 2 to 3 minutes, until the cheese has begun to melt and the bread is golden brown. Press down with a spatula, flip, and grill the second side. Remove from the pan onto a cutting board.

Allow the grilled sandwich to cool down for 5 minutes before packing in a lunch container.

Serve with ¼ cup (65 g) Homemade Salsa (page 114) for dipping.

Pretzelwich

My daughter says that everything tastes better in a pretzel roll. Her happy empty lunchbox proves it's true.

1 teaspoon mustard

2 teaspoons (9 g) mayonnaise

1 pretzel roll, sliced in half

2 slices (40 g) ham

1 slice (20 g) provolone cheese

Lettuce (optional)

Tomato (optional)

—

YIELD: 1 serving

Mix mustard and mayonnaise, and spread onto both sides of the roll. Layer the ham and cheese, top with the lettuce and tomato, if using, and close the pretzelwich.

Egg Salad Sandwich

I usually hard-boil about a half-dozen eggs at the beginning of the week and keep them in my fridge, just in case we need to assemble an extra lunch quickly, or add protein to a veggie-laden meal.

1 hard-boiled egg, mashed or chopped

2 teaspoons (10 g) plain Greek yogurt or mayonnaise

Dash of ground paprika

Salt and pepper

2 slices whole-grain bread

—

YIELD: 1 sandwich

In a small bowl, combine the egg, yogurt, and paprika until well combined. Season with the salt and pepper to taste.

Spread the egg salad on one of the bread slices, and close the sandwich.

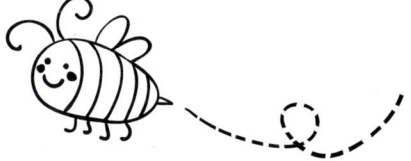

KITCHEN NOTE

I make this sandwich the night before. In the morning, I place it inside the freezer for 20 minutes while I get the kids ready. This extra cooling helps the egg salad stay cold inside the lunchbox, and I don't need to bother with extra ice packs.

< Angel Food Sandwich

The first time I made this sandwich, my daughter said: "Mom, I am quite sure this is what angels eat in heaven."

1½ tablespoons (23 g) whipped cream cheese

2 slices white wheat sandwich bread

½ small banana, sliced

1 or 2 strawberries, sliced

—
YIELD: 1 serving

Spread the cream cheese evenly on each slice of bread.

Layer with the banana and strawberries, and close the sandwich.

Candy Apple Sandwich

Healthier and more nutritious than the red-sugar coated ones and way less sticky!

2 tablespoons (32 g) Caramel Peanut Butter (page 107)

2 slices whole-grain bread

¼ apple, sliced thin

—
YIELD: 1 serving

Spread the peanut butter on both slices of bread. Lay the apple slices evenly over one of the slices, and close the sandwich.

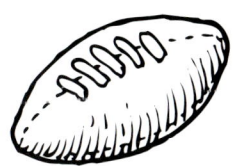

Honey Bee Sandwich

"Creamy, sweet, and delicious" is how my son describes this sandwich. Loaded with protein and whole grains, it makes this mom happy.

3 tablespoons (49 g) part-skim ricotta cheese

2 slices hearty oat bread, lightly toasted

1 teaspoon honey

—

YIELD: 1 serving

Spread the ricotta on one slice of bread and drizzle with the honey. Top with the other slice of bread.

Ricotta and Jam Pancake Sandwich >

Your kids will love opening up their lunchboxes and seeing that their sandwiches are made with pancakes.

3 tablespoons (28 g) part-skim ricotta cheese

4 Perfect Pancakes (page 9), 2-inch (5 cm) diameter

1 tablespoon (20 g) Easy Freezer Jam (page 106)

—

YIELD: 1 serving

Spread the ricotta evenly onto two of the pancakes; top with the jam, then top with the remaining pancakes.

LAURA'S TIP

Purchase a large tub of ricotta cheese and make the Midweek Penne Bake (page 86), and use the leftover ricotta for either sandwich on this page.

< Grilled Chicken and Pesto Sandwich

The combination of grilled chicken with fresh pesto works beautifully in this easy, yet savory grilled cheese sandwich. It takes leftover chicken to a whole new level!

Butter, for grilling

2 slices whole-grain bread

2 teaspoons (9 g) mayonnaise

2 teaspoons (10 g) Homemade Pesto (page 110)

2 ounces (40 g) cooked boneless chicken breast, sliced thin

1 slice (20 g) mozzarella cheese

—
YIELD: 1 serving

Butter one side of both bread slices; flip over onto a cutting board.

Spread the mayonnaise and pesto on both bread slices. Layer the chicken and mozzarella, and close the sandwich.

Place the sandwich, buttered side down, on a skillet over medium heat. Grill for 2 to 3 minutes, until the cheese has begun to melt and the bread is golden brown. Press down with a spatula, flip, and grill the second side.

Remove from the pan onto a cutting board. Slice in half, and serve immediately or allow the sandwich to cool prior to packing in a lunchbox.

Barbecue Chicken Sandwich

"Chicken isn't the same without barbecue sauce; it just tastes more plain," said my daughter one day. And just like that, this sandwich marked the end of plain chicken sandwiches for her.

4 ounces (113 g) oven roasted or grilled chicken, finely chopped

2 teaspoons (10 g) mayonnaise

2 teaspoons (10 g) barbecue sauce

Salt and pepper

2 slices whole-grain bread

Lettuce and tomato (optional)

—
YIELD: 1 serving

In a bowl, combine the chicken, mayonnaise, and barbecue sauce. Season with the salt and pepper to taste.

Spread the chicken salad on one slice of bread. Dress the sandwich with lettuce and tomato (if your kids prefer it that way), and close the sandwich.

LAURA'S TIP

Cook extra chicken one night this week. Assemble the chicken salad after dinner to save time in the morning.

Turkey and Hummus Sandwich

While I love this sandwich with all the fixings, my youngest prefers it plain and grilled. Either way, it's high in protein and full of flavor.

2 tablespoons (28 g) Greek Hummus (page 111)

2 slices whole-grain bread

2 slices (40 g) turkey

Lettuce leaves

Tomato slices

—
YIELD: 1 sandwich

On a cutting board, spread the hummus on one slice of the bread, top with the turkey, lettuce, and tomato. Close the sandwich.

Veggie Club >

This veggie club is certain to convince you that a traditional club sandwich is overrated.

3 slices whole-wheat sandwich bread

2 tablespoons (30 g) Greek Hummus (page 111)

½ medium steak tomato, sliced thin

2 slices (40 g) provolone cheese

1 tablespoon (15 g) Homemade Pesto (page 110)

—
YIELD: 1 or 2 servings

Lay all three bread slices on a cutting board. Spread half of the hummus onto one bread slice. Top with half of the tomato slices and one slice of cheese.

On the second slice of bread, spread half of the pesto and flip, pesto side down, to close the sandwich. Spread the remaining pesto on top of the second bread slice, and top with the remaining tomato slices and cheese. Spread the remaining hummus on the third bread slice and flip over to close the sandwich.

LAURA'S TIP

If you are making this sandwich the night before, place the turkey closest to the bread and the hummus in the middle. This will prevent the bread from getting soggy.

< Peaches and Cream Wafflewich

Waffles make the perfect sandwich bread, especially when the filling is sweet and creamy!

2 tablespoons (30 g) cream cheese
2 Whole Wheat Waffles (page 20)
1 peach, sliced thin

—
YIELD: 1 serving

Spread the cream cheese evenly on both waffles. Place the peach slices onto one of the waffles, and close the sandwich.

Sunny Side Sandwich

Sunshine and lemon bread are two things that make my son happy. The peanut butter and honey are just a bonus.

1½ tablespoons (8 g) peanut butter
2 slices Lemon Bread (page 100)
1 teaspoon honey

—
YIELD: 1 serving

Carefully spread the peanut butter on one bread slice. Drizzle with the honey, and close the sandwich.

Kid's Philly Steak Sandwich

This simple, satisfying sandwich is the perfect kid-friendly version of the classic Philly Cheesesteak.

2 tablespoons (30 g) whipped cream cheese

2 slices whole-grain bread

2 slices (40 g) roast beef, sliced thin

—

YIELD: 1 serving

Spread the cream cheese onto both slices of the bread. Top with the roast beef, and close the sandwich.

Easy Muffuletta >

While the traditional muffuletta is made with a veggie olive salad, this version is easier to make and a lot more kid friendly.

One 10-inch (25.5 cm) round Italian bread

1 cup (160 g) Olive Salad (page 110)

Extra-virgin olive oil (optional)

4 ounces (80 g) Genoa salami

4 ounces (80 g) capicola or deli ham

3 or 4 thin slices mozzarella

3 or 4 thin slices provolone cheese

—

YIELD: 4 servings

Cut the bread in half, lengthwise. Brush both cut sides with the oil from your olive salad, or the olive oil, if using, with more on the bottom half.

Begin layering the salami and ham on the bottom half of the bread. Top with the mozzarella and provolone cheese.

Next, add the olive salad from the center out. Place the other bread half on the top, and press it down without smashing the bread. Cut it into quarters.

For a school lunch: Wrap each quarter in parchment paper (or foil) to keep it together. Place inside a lunch bag.

LAURA'S TIP

This sandwich is also excellent grilled.

KITCHEN NOTE

You can toast or warm up the sandwich in your oven for a few minutes prior to cutting. Alternatively, you can use a long Italian bread loaf if a round one is not available.

< Avocado Delight

One of my mottos: Cream cheese makes everything taste better. When I'm trying to introduce a new flavor or previously not-favored fruit, veggie, or protein to my kids, I often try the cream cheese route. I've since stopped stressing about my kids not eating things raw or not wanting to try an unfamiliar food. If it has cream cheese, they will, at the very least, try it.

¼ avocado, mashed

2 slices whole wheat bread or 1 wrap

1 tablespoon (15 g) whipped cream cheese

2 slices ham

1 or 2 spinach leaves

Salt and pepper

—
YIELD: 1 serving

Spread the avocado on one slice of bread.

Spread the cream cheese on the other slice. Add the ham and spinach leaves. Season with the salt and pepper to taste, and close the sandwich.

Hummus Monster

If ballparks served a healthy sandwich, I think this would be it. It has all the classic pretzel and mustard flavors, but added nutrition thanks to the veggies and hummus.

1 round pretzel roll

1 teaspoon mustard

1 tablespoon (15 g) hummus

1 or 2 thin tomato slices

1 or 2 lettuce leaves

—
YIELD: 1 serving

On a cutting board, slice the roll in half. Spread the mustard thinly over both halves, and top with the hummus.

Layer the tomato and lettuce on one of the slices, and close the roll.

Pure Pastrami

A sandwich made for simple kids, such as my daughter, who loves the salty cured flavor of pastrami.

1 teaspoon mustard

2 teaspoons (9 g) mayonnaise

2 slices whole-grain bread

4 thin slices (80 g) pastrami

—
YIELD: 1 serving

Combine the mustard and mayonnaise in a small bowl.

Place the bread on a cutting board. Spread the mayonnaise mixture onto both slices. Layer the pastrami on one of the slices, and close the sandwich.

Hawaiian Sliders >

Bite-size, sweet, and delicious. These are a kid favorite!

1 teaspoon yellow mustard

2 teaspoons (9 g) mayonnaise

2 Hawaiian rolls

2 slices (40 g) ham

2 pineapple rings

—
YIELD: 1 serving

In a small bowl, combine the mustard and mayonnaise. Slice the rolls in half, and spread the mustard and mayonnaise thinly over each roll.

Cut the ham slices in half, then fold each half into quarters. Place a folded ham quarter over each roll half, top two of those with a pineapple ring, and top with other roll half to close the rolls.

< PB & J Pinwheels

This recipe takes the classic peanut butter and jelly for a spin.

2 whole-wheat bread slices

2 tablespoons (32 g) peanut butter

1 tablespoon (20 g) jelly

—

YIELD: 1 serving

Using a serrated knife, cut the crusts from the whole wheat bread slices. Flatten each slice with a rolling pin.

Spread the peanut butter and jelly on the prepared bread slices and roll tightly. Cut each roll in half and then into 1-inch (2.5 cm) pieces.

<Strawberry Fruit Leather

Who knew making fruit leather could be this simple? Feel free to experiment with your child's favorite fruit.

5 cups (850 g) strawberries, hulled and halved

2 tablespoons (42 g) honey

—

YIELD: 12 to 14 strips

Preheat the oven to the lowest temperature setting, which will probably be somewhere in between 150°F and 200°F (65°C and 93°C).

In a medium saucepan over low heat, cook the strawberries until they are soft and the juices begin to release. Add the honey and stir until combined.

Pour into a food processor or blender and purée. If your kids don't like the seeds, pour the mixture through a fine-mesh strainer.

Line a baking sheet with parchment paper, and pour the berry mixture onto the sheet. Bake for 4 to 6 hours, until the fruit leather peels away easily from the parchment. Once cooled, cut the fruit leather (with parchment) into strips.

KITCHEN NOTES

Don't pour too thin of a layer, or you'll have fruit crisps instead of fruit leather. If it's too thick, it will take longer to dehydrate. An even consistent layer in both color and thickness works best.

All oven temperatures vary, so begin checking after 3½ hours of baking, and remember: The center of the tray always takes longer than the edges.

Cuban Pinwheels

Craving a Cuban sandwich, but realizing we were out of bread, I resorted to my favorite go-to option—flour tortillas! This Cuban sandwich wrap is now a staple in our lunch rotation—it's fast, easy, and delicious!

One 8 -inch (20 cm) tortilla

2 slices (40 g) honey ham

2 slices (40 g) pastrami

2 slices (40 g) provolone cheese

—
YIELD: 1 serving

Layer the tortilla with the ham, pastrami, and cheese. Roll tightly. Cut the tortilla roll in half, and then into 1-inch (2.5 cm) rounds.

Optional: After layering the ingredients, transfer the tortilla into a skillet. Grill the tortilla open-faced for about 3 minutes on medium-low heat, remove from the pan, and roll.

Hawaiian Puff-Wheels >

My daughter loves finding these in her lunchbox. She says they are fancy and delicious. The variations are endless, so this one recipe can yield many happy lunchboxes for years to come.

1 package (17 ounces, or 490 g) puff pastry sheets, thawed

¾ cup (112 g) sliced deli ham, finely chopped

½ cup (80 g) crushed pineapple, well drained

1¼ cups (145 g) shredded Cheddar cheese

—
YIELD: 4 or 5 servings

Preheat the oven to 375°F (190°C), and line a baking sheet with parchment paper.

On a lightly floured surface, unroll the pastry sheets. Spread the ham and pineapple evenly over both sheets. Sprinkle with the cheese.

Carefully roll the dough, starting with the long side so that you end up with a long log. Cut the filled dough into 1-inch (2.5 cm) thick pieces, and place on the baking sheet.

Bake for 10 to 12 minutes until the dough rises and is golden. Remove from the oven, and allow the wheels to cool for 5 minutes prior to packing in a lunchbox. If you make these the night before, pack them chilled in the lunchbox. They will be room temperature by lunch.

RECIPE VARIATIONS

- ½ cup (80 g) crumbled bacon + 1¼ cups (150 g) Cheddar cheese
- ¼ cup (65 g) pesto sauce + ½ cup (75 g) crumbled feta + ½ cup (60 g) mozzarella cheese

< ABC Pinwheels

I love the combination of avocado and bacon. The sweet flavor of ripe avocado paired with the crunchy, salty flavor of bacon is definitely worth each savory bite.

¼ avocado, mashed

2 teaspoons (10 g) mayonnaise

One 8-inch (20 cm) flour tortilla

2 slices (15 g) bacon, cooked and crumbled

2 tablespoons (15 g) shredded, white Cheddar cheese

—
YIELD: 1 serving

In a small bowl, mash the avocado and mix with the mayonnaise.

Place the tortilla on a cutting board, and spread the mayonnaise–avocado mixture evenly over the top. Top with the bacon and cheese.

Roll the tortilla tightly. Cut the tortilla roll in half, and then into 1-inch (2.5 cm) pieces.

Tapenade Pinwheels

My daughter, the olive lover, often asks for extra olives on the side. Some weeks, she asks for this lunch twice.

One 8-inch (20 cm) flour tortilla

2 tablespoons (13 g) whipped cream cheese

¼ cup (25 g) Olive Salad (page 110)

—
YIELD: 1 serving

Place the tortilla on a cutting board and spread the cream cheese evenly over the tortilla. Top with the olive salad.

Roll the tortilla tightly. Cut the tortilla roll in half, and then into 1-inch (2.5 cm) pieces.

LAURA'S TIP

Save time in the morning by assembling pinwheels the night before and packing them in the lunchbox.

Chocolate Flautas

One weekend morning, I wanted to make chocolate crepes for my kids, but I had no eggs! Since the kids already had their mind set on crepes for breakfast, I substituted with whole-grain tortillas instead. The kids loved them, and they've since become a lunchbox favorite as well.

One 8-inch (20 cm) whole-grain flour tortilla

2 tablespoons (32 g) Easy Homemade Chocolate Spread (page 107)

½ cup (85 g) strawberries, sliced

—
YIELD: 1 serving

Lay the tortilla on a cutting board. Distribute the chocolate spread over the tortilla.

Beginning at one end, roll tightly. Cut the roll in half and secure with a bento pick or lunch skewer. Serve with the strawberries.

Honey Mustard Chicken Wrap

This wrap is hearty and filling and combines the great flavors of honey mustard and chicken, which kids love.

1 tablespoon (11 g) honey mustard

One 8-inch (20 cm) tortilla

2 slices (40 g) deli roasted chicken, or 2 ounces (40 g) cooked chicken, chopped

1 slice (20 g) Cheddar cheese

1 leaf green-leaf lettuce

¼ medium tomato, diced

—
YIELD: 1 serving

On a cutting board, spread the honey mustard over the tortilla, leaving a ½-inch (1.3 cm) rim all the way around.

Top the tortilla with the chicken, cheese, lettuce, and tomato. Roll tightly and cut in half.

LAURA'S TIP

If you store the flour tortillas in the fridge, give them a quick warm-up in the toaster oven or in a skillet over medium heat, just to take the chill off.

Crunchy Carrot Wrap

My daughter will only eat veggies when they are crunchy, which is a good thing because they are most nutritous that way. The addition of honey and ricotta adds a creamy sweetness that makes raw veggies irresistible for kids and adults alike!

One 8-inch (20 cm) tortilla

2 tablespoons (30 g) ricotta cheese

¼ cup (28 g) carrots, finely shredded

2 teaspoons (14 g) honey

½ teaspoon grated lemon peel

—

YIELD: 1 serving

Lay the tortilla on a cutting board. Spread the ricotta over the tortilla, leaving a ½-inch (1.3 cm) rim at the edges. Layer the carrots evenly. Drizzle with the honey and top with the lemon peel. Roll tightly, and cut the wrap in half.

Little Italy Wrap

It's like a pizza, but wrapped—and fast!

One 8-inch (20 cm) tortilla

5 thin slices (100 g) salami

2 slices (40 g) mozzarella cheese

1 Roma tomato, finely diced

—

YIELD: 1 serving

Lay the tortilla on a cutting board. Layer the salami and cheese evenly. Top with the tomato. Roll tightly, and cut the wrap in half.

All My Veggies Wrap

It can be hard to get kids to eat salad, but in this wrap, they won't even notice they are eating lots of veggies! The pesto also provides a boost of nutrition.

1 tablespoon (15 g) Homemade Pesto (page 110)

One 8-inch (20 cm) tortilla

2 or 3 butterhead lettuce leaves

¼ cup (28 g) carrots, shredded

¼ cucumber, julienned

—

YIELD: 1 serving

On a cutting board, spread the pesto over the tortilla. Layer the lettuce leaves, and top with the carrots and cucumber. Roll tightly and cut in half.

Turkey Avocado Wrap

When in doubt: wrap, pack, and serve.

One 8-inch (20 cm) spinach wrap

1 tablespoon (15 g) plain Greek yogurt

¼ teaspoon Arriba! Seasoning (page 58)

¼ avocado, diced

3 slices (60 g) oven roasted turkey

¼ cup (65 g) Homemade Salsa (page 114)

—

YIELD: 1 serving

Lay the wrap on a cutting board and spread with the yogurt. Sprinkle with the seasoning, then layer the avocado and turkey.

Roll tightly and cut in half. Pack the salsa in a small container with a lid.

Pizza Dough Stromboli

The debate is out there about where to get the best stromboli in any given city. For my family, however, the best comes straight out of my oven.

1 Pizza Dough (page 103)

1 cup (150 g) mozzarella cheese, grated and divided

¼ cup (25 g) grated Parmesan cheese + additional for topping

½ cup (125 g) pizza sauce or Veggie Tomato Sauce (page 84) + additional for dipping

¼ pound (60 g) Genoa salami

¼ pound (60 g) honey ham

1 egg, beaten

—
YIELD: 4 to 6 servings

Make the pizza dough following the recipe directions.

Preheat the oven to 500°F (250°C). Line a baking sheet with parchment paper, and set aside.

In a small bowl, combine the cheeses. Roll out the pizza dough onto the baking sheet to approximately 10 × 16 inches (25 × 40.6 cm). Spread the sauce over two-thirds of the dough lengthwise, leaving about 3 inches (7.5 cm) of plain dough along one of the edges.

Top the sauce with half of the cheese mix, then the salami and ham, and then the remaining cheese mix.

Brush the plain strip of dough with the egg. Roll up into a log, lengthwise, starting with the end filled with toppings and ending with the plain strip of dough at the bottom of the roll. Pinch the ends or tuck them in.

Lightly coat the entire stromboli with egg. Cut slats on the top of the dough every 2 inches (5 cm), so that steam can escape. Sprinkle with the additional Parmesan cheese, and bake for 12 to 14 minutes or until golden brown.

Allow the stromboli to cool for 5 minutes before slicing into pieces. Serve with the additional sauce.

For a school lunch: In the morning, lightly warm up a piece of stromboli in a toaster oven or regular oven. Store pizza sauce in a small leak-proof container, and pack in the lunchbox. Stromboli is great at room temperature.

Pizza Dippers

My friend, Kendra Peterson, has a way of repurposing leftovers so that they don't look the same as the original dish. She took pizza slices and created the dippers.

2 slices leftover pizza

¼ cup (62 g) Veggie Tomato Sauce (page 84)

—
YIELD: 1 serving

Cut leftover pizza into thin strips. Serve with the tomato sauce.

LAURA'S TIP

Avoid messy lunch bags by making sure you store pizza sauce in a leak-proof container.

Green Eggs and Ham Pizza

Your family will beg for that single leftover slice; so you might as well double the recipe and make more for everyone. That way, you have something to pack for lunch!

1 Pizza Dough (page 103)

1 cup (245 g) pizza sauce or Veggie Tomato Sauce (page 84)

2½ cups (290 g) shredded mozzarella cheese

4 hard-boiled eggs, chopped

8 ounces (160 g) sliced honey ham, chopped

½ cup (50 g) green olives, sliced

—
YIELD: 6 servings

Prepare the pizza dough, following the recipe directions, and preheat the oven to 375°F (190°C).

Using a rolling pin, roll out one of the dough balls onto a floured surface. Transfer it to a floured baking sheet.

Spread half of the pizza sauce on to the base, leaving a ½-inch (1.3 cm) border all the way around. Layer half of the cheese over the sauce and begin to distribute half of the toppings evenly: eggs, ham, and olives. Repeat the process with the second dough ball and the remaining ingredients.

Bake the pizzas in the oven for about 22 to 25 minutes, until the edges are golden and have risen. Remove from the oven.

Cheddar and Pear Quesadillas

This creative quesadilla inspired my daughter to enjoy pears. The tangy sharp Cheddar cheese paired with sweet ripe pears creates a wonderful flavor combination that kids of all ages enjoy!

1 tablespoon (14 g) mayonnaise

2 teaspoons (8 g) mustard

Two 8-inch (20 cm) flour tortillas

1 small pear, sliced thin

⅓ cup (38 g) shredded sharp Cheddar cheese

Oil for grilling

—

YIELD: 2 servings

In a small dish, mix the mayonnaise and mustard.

Spread a thin layer of the mayo–mustard spread over each tortilla. Spread the pear over one tortilla, sprinkle the cheese over the pear, and then top with the second tortilla, mayo-mustard side down.

Brush the bottom side of the tortilla with oil, and grill in a 10-inch (25 cm) skillet over medium heat until the cheese is melted, about 2 to 3 minutes. Brush the top of the tortilla with oil, and flip to grill the other side.

Baked Raviolis

There is a popular restaurant that serves fried raviolis as an appetizer. My daughter tried them once and loved them. Not wanting to eat fried foods at home (not to mention the mess of frying anything), I decided to bake them instead. This recipe was an all-around success!

1½ cups (175 g) plain Panko bread crumbs

¾ cup (90 g) plain bread crumbs

¼ teaspoon salt

2 teaspoons (4 g) Italian seasoning

1 tablespoon (5 g) grated Parmesan cheese

3 eggs, beaten

24 frozen cheese raviolis

Olive oil spray

—
YIELD: 24 baked raviolis

Preheat the oven to 425°F (220°C), and line a large baking sheet with parchment paper.

In a shallow bowl, mix the bread crumbs, salt, Italian seasoning, and Parmesan cheese. In a large bowl, beat the eggs. Set aside.

In a medium saucepan, bring water to a boil, cook the raviolis for 3 minutes, drain and allow them to cool for 5 for 10 minutes.

Begin the breading process by adding 4 raviolis at a time to the beaten eggs, and flip to coat. Transfer to the Parmesan and bread-crumb mixture, and toss to coat well. Place on the baking sheet.

Repeat the breading process with the remaining ravioli. Coat lightly with the olive oil spray and bake for 15 minutes.

Serve with ¼ cup (60 g) Veggie Tomato Sauce (page 84).

For a school lunch: Make these ravioli for dinner the night before. Double this recipe if necessary. In the morning, lightly warm the ravioli and pack in a lunchbox. They are meant to be eaten at room temperature.

LAURA'S TIP

This is an easy recipe for your kids to help make. Little hands can help bread extra raviolis. Freeze them and pull them out when you need them.

Pesto Pasta

This pasta is the base for many delicious lunches. Add veggies, chicken, or sundried tomatoes for a complete meal.

1 box (16 ounces, or 454 g) elbow or rotini pasta

½ cup (130 g) Homemade Pesto (page 110)

2 teaspoons (10 ml) lemon juice

½ cup (115 g) Greek yogurt

—
YIELD: 8 servings

Cook the pasta according to the package directions, drain and set aside.

In a large bowl, combine the pesto, lemon juice, and yogurt. Fold the pasta into the pesto until all the pasta is evenly coated. Serve warm or cold.

For a school lunch: Fill a preheated thermos with warm pasta, or pack inside a lunch container to be eaten cold.

Garden Fresh Pasta

Is it a salad? Is it a pasta bowl? It's both! Colorful, fresh, nutritious, and the perfect way to use leftovers!

¾ cup (105 g) cooked pasta

2 teaspoons (30 g) Homemade Pesto (page 110)

¼ cup (56 g) chopped fresh baby spinach

¼ cup (38 g) cherry tomatoes, halved

½ carrot, grated

1 teaspoon grated Parmesan cheese

—
YIELD: 1 serving

Mix all ingredients in a bowl until the pesto is thoroughly distributed.

LAURA'S TIP

Make this after dinner with leftover cooked pasta and refrigerate overnight in the lunchbox container. In the morning it's grab-and-go!

Greek Orzo Pasta Salad

This simple salad is filling, delicious, and full of Mediterranean flavor.

⅔ cup (75 g) whole wheat orzo pasta

1½ tablespoons (25 ml) olive oil

2 cups (60 g) baby spinach, chopped

½ cup (75 g) crumbled feta cheese

⅓ cup (48 g) raisins

¼ cup (25 g) finely chopped pitted black olives

2 tablespoons (30 ml) fresh lemon juice

Salt and pepper

—

YIELD: 4 servings

Cook orzo according to package instructions, drain and empty into a bowl.

Toss the orzo with olive oil and mix it well to combine. Add the spinach, feta cheese, raisins, olives, lemon juice, and season with the salt and pepper to taste.

Italian Pasta Salad

This easy-to-make pasta dish is one of my daughter's favorite lunches. It tastes just like pizza—a kid favorite for sure!

¾ cup (105 g) cooked pasta

4 or 5 slices pepperoni, chopped

2 ounces (40 g) mozzarella, cubed small

1½ tablespoons (15 g) black olives, sliced

¼ cup (45 g) cherry tomatoes, halved

2 teaspoons (30 ml) olive oil

Salt and pepper

—

YIELD: 1 serving

In a bowl, combine all ingredients, adding salt and pepper to taste. Mix well until the oil evenly coats the salad.

Neighborhood Meatballs

This is one of the first recipes my good friend Melissa shared with me when I moved into the neighborhood. It's a family favorite and a staple in both our homes.

FOR MEATBALLS:

4 ounces (120 g) Saltine crackers, finely crushed

1 pound (450 g) ground turkey or beef

½ pound (225 g) ground turkey sausage

¼ cup (6 g) parsley

3 eggs, beaten

2 teaspoons (6 g) garlic powder

½ teaspoon salt

1 teaspoon black pepper

¼ cup (25 g) grated Parmesan cheese

FOR RED GRAVY:

3 tablespoons (45 ml) olive oil

1 small onion

2 cloves garlic, chopped

1 teaspoon salt

1 teaspoon black pepper

2 tablespoons (8 g) oregano

1 tablespoon (5 g) basil

3 cans (28 ounces, or 2.4 kg) crushed tomatoes

1 tablespoon (13 g) sugar

—

YIELD: 8 servings

Preheat the oven to 400°F (200°C).

To make the meatballs: In a large bowl, combine the saltine crumbs, meat, parsley, eggs, garlic, salt, pepper, and Parmesan cheese. Mix with your hands until everything is evenly combined.

With your hands, form 24 meatballs. Place each meatball into a greased baking pan, cover with foil, and cook for 15 minutes. Flip them after 15 minutes, and remove the foil for the next 15 minutes.

To make the red gravy: While the meatballs are cooking, heat the olive oil over medium-high heat in an 8-quart (7.6 L) soup pot.

Add the onion and cook for 3 to 5 minutes, stirring occasionally, until translucent. Add the garlic, salt, pepper, oregano, and basil, and cook for a minute or two. Pour in the tomatoes and sugar. Stir, bring to a boil, and reduce the heat.

When the meatballs are done, carefully take them out and place them in the red gravy. Cook for an additional 30 to 45 minutes with the cover on to blend all the flavors.

LAURA'S TIP

This recipe yields extra red gravy (or tomato sauce) and will be perfect for other dinners or lunches!

6 to 8 small Neighborhood Meatballs (page 56)

3 or 4 thin slices (60 to 80 g) Parmesan Crostinis (page 104)

½ cup (123 g) tomato sauce from Neighborhood Meatballs

—

YIELD: 1 serving

Meatball Dippers

Remember my awesome Neighborhood Meatballs your family loved for dinner? These fun dippers are hearty, filling, and one lunch option your kids will love.

Skewer or place the meatballs in a lunch container. Pour and store warmed sauce in a leak-proof container or thermos. In a separate compartment or container, store crostinis.

Olives and Feta Lego Pasta

One peek inside her thermos, and my daughter gets so excited when she finds this yummy pasta waiting for her. Good thing, because it's an easy dinner that yields leftovers!

1 pound (454 g) ditalini pasta

½ cup (120 ml) olive oil

1 lemon, juiced

1 can (6 ounces, or 170 g) whole black olives

One 4-ounce container (75 g) crumbled feta cheese

Kosher salt and freshly cracked black pepper

—
YIELD: 6 servings

Bring a large pot of salted water to a boil over high heat. Add the pasta; reduce the heat, and cook until al dente, according to the package instructions, and drain.

While the pasta is cooking, in a medium bowl, whisk together the olive oil and lemon juice. Toss in the olives and feta.

Once the pasta is cooked, transfer it to the bowl. Toss all ingredients together until well combined. Add salt and pepper to taste, and serve.

For a school lunch: Warm the pasta leftovers and transfer to a preheated thermos.

Arriba! Seasoning

Very similar to taco seasoning, but with a smoky flavor, less spice, and a whole lot of kid appeal.

3 tablespoons (23 g) chili powder

2 tablespoons (14 g) ground cumin

1 tablespoon (7 g) ground paprika

1½ teaspoons salt

2 teaspoons (4 g) black pepper

2 teaspoons (6 g) garlic powder

1 teaspoon onion powder

2 teaspoons (2 g) dried oregano

—
YIELD: 9 tablespoons (69 g)

In a small bowl, combine all ingredients. Store in an airtight container.

Veggie Meat Loaf

"Mom! There's green and orange stuff in here!" Oh, the confetti sprinkles you mean?

1 cup (130 g) carrots,
finely chopped

½ zucchini (60 g), chopped

1 handful spinach,
finely chopped

½ onion, chopped

2 cloves garlic, chopped

1 cup (115 g) bread crumbs

1 tablespoon (2 g)
Italian seasoning

½ teaspoon black pepper

1½ pounds (340 g) ground
turkey or beef

2 eggs

1 can (8 ounces, or 245 g)
tomato sauce

3 tablespoons (48 g)
barbecue sauce

—
YIELD: 6 servings

Preheat the oven to 325°F (170 °C), and lightly grease a 9-inch (23 cm) loaf pan.

In a food processor or mini chopper, chop the carrots, zucchini, spinach, onion, and garlic until finely chopped. Place in a large bowl.

Add the bread crumbs, Italian seasoning, pepper, turkey, and eggs. Using your hands, combine the ingredients until they are all well mixed.

Pack the mixture into the loaf pan. Combine the tomato sauce and barbecue sauce, and pour over the meat mixture.

Bake for 1 hour to 1 hour 15 minutes. Oven times and temperatures will vary, so check for doneness after 50 minutes by using an instant-read thermometer. Turkey is cooked at 165°F (74°C), and beef at 160°F (71°C).

< Grilled Cheese Dippers

My daughter says "dipping is a lot more fun when cheese is involved." You know what? I must admit that I agree with her.

Butter, for grilling

2 slices whole-grain bread

2 slices (40 g) white Cheddar cheese

—
YIELD: 1 serving

Butter one side of both bread slices; flip over onto a cutting board. Place the cheese on one slice of the bread and close the sandwich with the second slice.

Place the cheese sandwich, buttered side down, on a skillet over medium heat. Grill for 2 to 3 minutes, until the cheese has begun to melt, and the bread is golden brown. Press down with a spatula, flip, and grill the second side. Remove onto a cutting board.

Allow the sandwich to cool for 5 minutes, cut into narrow strips, and pack in a lunch container.

For a school lunch: Try serving it with Tomato Veggie Soup (page 90).

KITCHEN NOTE

Let the grilled sandwich cool down before slicing and packing it in the lunchbox. If you cut it too soon and pack it while it's still hot, the bread will be soggy by lunchtime.

Spaghetti Tacos

If your kids like "all things crunchy" like mine do, these spaghetti tacos are certain to be a lunchbox favorite. It's a crazy combo, but kids love it.

2 hard taco shells

1 cup (140 g) leftover spaghetti mixed with Veggie Tomato Sauce (page 84)

1 tablespoon (5 g) Parmesan cheese

—
YIELD: 1 serving

Warm the taco shells in a toaster oven. Lightly warm the spaghetti.

Fill each taco shell with ½ cup (70 g) spaghetti. Sprinkle with the cheese.

For a school lunch: Pack spaghetti tacos in a big-enough lunch container so that they are able to lay flat. Otherwise, consider sending spaghetti separately, and have your child stuff the taco.

Olive Strips

These flavorful sandwich strips taste just like Mediterranean pizza—but without all the work!

1½ tablespoons (25 g) cream cheese

2 slices whole-grain bread

1 tablespoon (10 g) Olive Salad (page 110)

—

YIELD: 1 serving

Spread the cream cheese on both slices of bread. Distribute the olive salad on one slice of the bread, and close the sandwich. Cut vertically into strips.

Lunchbox Falafels >

I love the versatility of these falafels. Easy to make and great to eat at room temperature, they're perfect to have in the fridge (or uncooked in the freezer) for a convenient and healthy lunch.

½ cup (375 g) dry chickpeas, soaked overnight, or 1 cup (240 g) canned chickpeas

2 teaspoons (14 g) ground cumin

½ teaspoon ground coriander

1 or 2 cloves garlic, minced

1 parsley sprig, minced

1 small onion, chopped fine

1½ tablespoons (45 ml) freshly squeezed lemon juice

3 tablespoons (21 g) bread crumbs

—

YIELD: 12 to 15 falafels

Drain and rinse the chickpeas that were soaking overnight, or rinse the canned chickpeas.

In a food processor, pulse the chickpeas with all the ingredients until it becomes a smooth thick paste.

With wet hands, form the dough into small balls, the size of a large walnut. Press down to form 1½-inch (3.8 cm) patties. If the mixture is too sticky, add a little more bread crumbs. If it's too dry, add a tablespoon (15 ml) or two of water.

Cook the falafels in an oiled pan over medium-high heat for 3 to 4 minutes each side, or until brown. Remove onto a paper towel–lined plate.

Serve with Greek Yogurt Dip (page 112).

For a school lunch: In the morning, toast the falafels in a toaster oven, baking oven, or a pan. Pack inside a lunch container.

Easy Peasy Frittata

I used to think frittatas were difficult to make because they sounded so fancy. This couldn't be further from the truth! They are easy to make and don't require flipping—which, for someone as messy as I am in the kitchen, is a good thing.

10 large eggs

⅓ cup (80 ml) milk

½ teaspoon salt

1 cup (130 g) frozen green peas

½ cup (58 g) shredded, sharp Cheddar cheese

2 tablespoons (28 g) butter

—
YIELD: 6 servings

In a medium bowl, combine the eggs, milk, and salt. Whisk until well blended. Mix in the frozen peas and cheese.

In a 12-inch (30.5 cm) skillet, melt the butter over medium-low heat. Swirl the pan around to evenly distribute the butter over the entire bottom and sides of pan.

Pour the egg mixture into the pan and, using a rubber spatula, give the mixture a quick stir to distribute the peas evenly.

Turn the heat to low. Allow the egg mixture to cook without stirring, about 5 minutes. Meanwhile, preheat your oven's broiler. Once the edges are cooked, and the center and top are still semiliquid, transfer the skillet to the broiler and continue to cook until the top and center are fully cooked, about 4 minutes.

Remove from the oven, and allow the frittata to cool before slicing.

For a school lunch: Place one slice of frittata inside of a lunchbox.

LAURA'S TIP

Remember to use an oven mitt when removing the pan from the oven. It will be quite hot! This lunch can be made ahead of time, stored in the refrigerator for up to three days, and enjoyed at room temperature.

CHAPTER THREE

Add Some Fun: Interactive Lunches for Picky Eaters

Kids love playing with their food, and healthy food should be fun to eat! This section helps you to find ways to sneak in more veggies, to re-create some of those packaged lunches from the store using healthy ingredients, and to introduce new foods in fun and interactive ways. Kids also love to assemble their own lunches, and this section will help to inspire both of you. Remember that most of the time you'll need to introduce a food in several different ways in order for your child to learn to love it. Do your best and the recipes in this book will take care of the rest.

< Veggie Skewers

Stick veggies on a "sword," and you'll be surprised that this just might be the trick to get them to eat their veggies!

⅓ cup (50 g) cherry tomatoes
¼ cup (40 g) fresh mini mozzarella balls
⅓ avocado, pitted and cubed
½ tablespoon (8 g) Homemade Pesto (page 110)
¼ cup (56 g) Greek Hummus (page 111)
2 or 3 Parmesan Crostinis (page 104)

—
YIELD: 1 serving

Using rounded-edge skewers or bento picks, alternate skewering tomatoes, mozzarella, and avocados. In two small lidded containers, pack the pesto and hummus.

Assemble all items in a compartmentalized lunch container, making sure the crostinis are in their own compartment.

Tortellini Swords

Last night's leftover tortellini becomes an easy-to-eat and delicious lunch.

½ cup (70 g) cooked tortellini
½ cup (75 g) cherry tomatoes
¼ cup (25 g) black olives

—
YIELD: 1 serving

Using rounded-edge skewers or bento picks, alternate skewering tortellini, tomatoes, cheese, and olives.

Alternatively, if you don't have skewers, mix all ingredients in a bowl. Drizzle with olive oil, and make it into a salad.

LAURA'S TIP

Add cubed mozzarella cheese if it's a family favorite.

Build Your Own Roman Army Boats

For the kid who won't eat chicken Caesar salad, because Roman Army Boats are a lot more fun.

⅓ cup (47 g) oven-roasted chicken, chopped

1 hard-boiled egg, chopped

1 tablespoon (15 ml) Caesar dressing

1 tablespoon (5 g) grated Parmesan cheese

4 to 6 hearts of romaine leaves

—
YIELD: 1 serving

In a small bowl, combine the chicken, egg, and dressing. Sprinkle with the cheese. Serve on the lettuce leaves.

For a school lunch: There are two ways to pack this lunch. Make the salad, pack it in a small container with a lid, and pack the lettuce leaves separately. The second option is to preassemble the lettuce cups in a rectangular lunchbox.

Ham and Cheese Swords >

My daughter loves swords. The ingredient possibilities are endless but oftentimes, she requests the most basic, yet her favorite, combination.

3 slices (60 g) honey ham

2 ounces (40 g) Cheddar cheese, cubed

6 to 8 whole-grain crackers

—
YIELD: 1 serving

On a cutting board, roll the ham tightly. Slice it into ½-inch (1.3 cm) pieces.

Alternate skewering the ham and cheese through toothpicks or bento picks.

For a school lunch: Serve the swords with whole-grain crackers, fresh fruit, and veggies.

KITCHEN NOTE

This is a great lunch to pack ahead of time. Make sure you store whole-grain crackers in a separate compartment or container so that they do not absorb moisture from the other food items.

LAURA'S TIP

For bigger appetites, shred romaine leaves and stuff them inside a pita.

< Mini Quiches

Easy, portable, perfectly portioned—all the things kids love in a tiny bite. Mix up the "add ins," and this recipe yields hundreds of options.

6 eggs

¼ cup (60 g) plain Greek yogurt

3 tablespoons (45 ml) milk

½ cup (75 g) ham, diced

1 cup (120 g) shredded Cheddar cheese

¼ teaspoon salt

¼ teaspoon black pepper

—
YIELD: 24 mini quiches

Preheat the oven to 350°F (180°C) and grease a mini muffin pan.

In a large bowl, whisk the eggs, yogurt, and milk. Add the ham, cheese, salt, and pepper.

Distribute the mixture evenly into the pan. Bake for 15 to 18 minutes. Allow the quiches to cool in the pan before carefully removing with a small knife or spatula.

For a school lunch: In the morning, reheat the quiches or pack cold. They will be room temperature by lunch.

Build Your Own Parfait

Your kids will be the envy of the lunch table with this lunch!

1 cup (230 g) low-fat vanilla yogurt

½ cup (75 g) mixed berries (sliced strawberries and blueberries)

1 tablespoon (5 g) Lunchbox Granola (page 20)

1 Whole Wheat Waffle (page 20)

—
YIELD: 1 serving

Pour the yogurt inside a chilled thermos. Top with the berries, and sprinkle with the granola. Close the thermos.

For a school lunch: Serve the parfait with a waffle with a side of maple syrup, Easy Freezer Jam (page 106), or White Chocolate Peanut Butter (page 109).

LAURA'S TIP

Store a clean thermos without the lid inside your freezer for quick preparation. Alternatively, chill the thermos for 15 minutes in the freezer or overnight.

Old School Cracker Stackers

Sometimes, kids find lunchbox joy in the simplest of things. For my son, it's licking the peanut butter and jelly after he twists these crackers open.

2 tablespoons (32 g) peanut butter

1 tablespoon (20 g) Easy Freezer Jam (page 106)

12 whole wheat round crackers

—

YIELD: 1 serving

Spread peanut butter and jam on half of the crackers, close into a cracker sandwich.

The Original MOMable >

This is the school lunch that started my own lunch revolution and built an entire community of parents who want fresh lunches for their kids. Easy to make, a kid favorite, and mine uses real ingredients.

2 ounces (40 g) white Cheddar cheese

2 slices (40 g) ham or turkey

8 whole-grain crackers

Strawberry Fruit Leather (page 41)

—

YIELD: 1 serving

On a cutting board, cut the cheese into thin square pieces. Cut the ham in half, and fold into quartered pieces.

For a school lunch: Assemble all the ingredients in a lunchbox, making sure the crackers are in their own compartment so that they do not absorb moisture and get soggy. Add fresh fruit or veggies.

LAURA'S TIP

This is the perfect lunch for a rushed morning of when you have nothing left to pack, or you've run out of bread and everything else. Serve along with yogurt, fruit, and veggies for a complete lunch.

< Peach Cobbler Box

This lunchbox reminds me of summer, all year long.

½ cup (125 g) ricotta cheese

1 teaspoon honey

1 fresh peach, sliced

2 tablespoons (15 g) granola

4 graham crackers

—

YIELD: 1 serving

Drizzle the ricotta with honey and top with the peaches.

Pack in a leak-proof container, or two separate leak-proof containers.

Store the granola and graham crackers separately, so that the dry ingredients do not get soggy by absorbing moisture from the wet ingredients.

Monkey Hot Dog

It looks like a hot dog, but it's not! Fun, meat-free, and quick to assemble—these are just a few of the reasons this lunch is a winner!

1 whole-grain hot dog bun

2 tablespoons (32 g) peanut butter

1 banana

1 tablespoon (20 g) Easy Freezer Jam (page 106)

—

YIELD: 1 hot dog

Spread the bun with the peanut butter and top with the banana. Spread the jam over the banana.

LAURA'S TIP

Don't have fresh peaches? Use ½ cup (125 g) frozen peach slices.

KITCHEN NOTE

Spread peanut butter and jelly on a hot dog bun, and pack an unpeeled banana in the lunchbox. Let your child assemble the hot dog at lunch.

Quinoa Bites

These meat-free high-protein bites are perfect for nugget-loving kids.

½ cup (86 g) quinoa

1 cup (235 ml) broth or stock

2 cups (180 g) oat flour

½ cup (28 g) finely chopped fresh spinach

1 cup (110 g) finely grated carrots

½ cup (50 g) grated Parmesan cheese

1 egg

¼ cup (60 ml) olive oil

⅓ cup (80 ml) milk

1½ teaspoons baking powder

—

YIELD: 10 bites

Cook the quinoa in the broth according to the package directions. Allow it to cool.

In a large bowl, combine the oat flour and quinoa. Add the spinach and carrots, and toss to combine.

In a medium-size bowl, mix the cheese, egg, olive oil, milk, and baking powder. Pour into the quinoa–veggie mixture. Mix until a thick batter is formed.

Preheat the oven to 350°F (180°C). Line a standard-size cupcake pan with paper liners (or grease the sides well) and fill each about halfway full with batter. Bake for 20 to 25 minutes, until golden brown. Remove from the oven, and allow the bites to cool slightly before serving.

Pesto Lover's Box >

When my youngest (at seventeen months of age) began dipping everything in my home-made pesto, I began creating pesto "boxes" for lunch. So simple, fresh, and delicious!

¼ cup (65 g) Homemade Pesto (page 110)

¼ cup (57 g) whole ripe olives

½ cup (75 g) cherry tomatoes

2 ounces (30 g) mozzarella cheese, cubed

2 or 3 Parmesan Crostinis (page 104)

—

YIELD: 1 serving

Assemble all the ingredients in a large lunchbox container, making sure that the pesto sauce is stored in a separate small leak-proof container.

CHAPTER FOUR

Fill the Thermos: Portable Hot Lunches

A thermos container will allow you to reuse leftovers and send hot foods to school. Start by preheating the thermos. To preheat, bring water to a boil (either on the stovetop on in the microwave), fill the thermos container with the hot water, and let it sit for about five minutes. Then, pour out the hot water and fill it with heated leftovers. Remember that you are warming up the leftovers to be eaten 3 to 5 hours later. The contents will need to be heated to a boil, on the stove, or piping hot in the microwave prior to placing them inside the thermos. In this section, I share some of my family's favorite recipes. Most of which yield leftovers your kids will love packed for lunch.

Tuna Quinoa Casserole

Creamy, cheesy, and full of flavor, this is one of the few ways my kids have tolerated quinoa.

1 cup (173 g) quinoa, dry

2 cups (470 g) vegetable stock

2 tablespoons (28 g) butter

2 tablespoons (16 g) flour

1 cup (120 ml) half and half or whole milk

1 cup (120 g) shredded, sharp Cheddar cheese

1 cup (115 g) mozzarella cheese, shredded

½ cup (40 g) Parmesan cheese, shredded

¼ teaspoon salt

¼ teaspoon black pepper

½ teaspoon ground cumin

1 cup (156 g) broccoli florets, thawed and finely chopped

½ cup (65 g) frozen corn

1 can (6 ounces, or 170 g) water-packed tuna, drained

—
YIELD: 6 servings

Preheat the oven to 350°F (180°C).

Cook the quinoa in the vegetable stock by bringing it to a boil, reducing the heat, and simmering for 15 minutes, or until all liquid has been absorbed.

While the quinoa is cooking, melt the butter over medium heat in a large skillet. Add the flour, and whisk continuously for a couple of minutes until the mixture thickens. Slowly pour in the half and half, and whisk to combine while removing any lumps.

In a small bowl, combine the cheeses. Reserve half of the cheese, and add the rest to the pan slowly while stirring. Once the cheese is melted, add the salt, pepper, and cumin.

When the quinoa is done, add the quinoa to the cheese sauce. Stir in the broccoli, corn, and tuna.

Pour the quinoa into a casserole dish. Top with the reserved cheese, and bake for 12 minutes or until the cheese is melted and bubbly.

For a school lunch: Fill a preheated thermos with warmed casserole.

LAURA'S TIP

Add 1 to 2 tablespoons (15 to 30 ml) of milk when heating up leftovers. It helps revive the sauce.

Dad's Fried Rice

My friend Jim is not only a father of two but also a fried rice connoisseur. He says there are no measurements to follow when making fried rice, just some simple rules, such as use leftover rice, don't skip the egg, add lots of "stuff" and be sure to make fried rice in a particular order. This recipe is easy and enables you to add a lot of delicious add-ins—a great way to utilize leftover veggies!

1 tablespoon (15 ml) vegetable oil

1 large egg, beaten

2 strips bacon, chopped

½ cup (70 g) cooked chicken, diced

1 cup (130 g) Asian stir-fry vegetables or 1 cup (130 g) peas, carrots, and baby corn mix, thawed

1 to 2 teaspoons (5 to 10 ml) soy or fish sauce

2 cups (330 g) cooked rice

—
YIELD: 3 servings

In a large skillet, heat the oil over medium-high heat. Add the egg. Let it sit until it begins to bubble and an omelet forms. Flip over, and cook until done. Then, transfer to a small bowl.

Add the bacon to the skillet. Cook for 5 to 7 minutes, stirring occasionally. When the bacon pieces are cooked, add the chicken. Then add the vegetables and soy sauce, and cook for a couple of minutes until everything is warmed through.

Finally, add the rice and egg. Thoroughly mix everything together. Once the rice and egg are evenly distributed and seared, turn off the heat and serve.

Bombay Rice >

My aunt made this rice for me, and I immediately loved the sweet and tangy flavors. So I asked her to write the recipe down for me to share. It's both delicious hot in a thermos, or served room temperature in a lunchbox.

1½ cups (360 ml) water

½ cup (120 ml) orange juice

1 cup (195 g) rice

¼ cup (60 g) pineapple chunks

⅓ cup (27 g) unsweetened, shredded coconut

⅓ cup (40 g) nuts, chopped, or ⅓ cup (48 g) raisins (optional)

—
YIELD: 4 servings

Bring the water and juice to a boil, then add the rice and raisins. Lower the heat, cover, and simmer until all the liquid is absorbed, about 20 minutes.

With a fork, fluff the rice and fold in the pineapple chunks and coconut. Mix in the nuts or raisins, if using.

< Margarita Pasta Salad

This salad is simple and delicious. Just like a Margarita pizza but with pasta!

¾ cup (102 g) cooked pasta

1 tablespoon (2.5 g) minced basil

¼ cup (45 g) cherry tomatoes, halved

2 teaspoons (30 ml) olive oil

Salt and pepper

—
YIELD: 1 serving

In a large bowl, combine all the ingredients. Mix well until the oil evenly coats the pasta. Season with the salt and pepper to taste.

Homemade Alfredo Sauce

Who knew that making your own Alfredo sauce was this easy! Ditch the jarred stuff and save money and increase nutrition with this homemade version. In fact, you probably already have all the ingredients on hand!

—
YIELD: About 2¾ cups (534 g)

½ cup (112 g) butter

2 cups (475 ml) half and half or whole milk

2 teaspoons (6 g) garlic powder

2 tablespoons (15 g) cream cheese

½ cup (50 g) grated Parmesan cheese

Bring the butter, half and half, garlic, and cream cheese to a boil while stirring often. Turn down the heat, simmer, and stir for about 2 minutes.

Add the Parmesan, and stir until melted. Simmer the sauce (on your smallest burner) for 15 to 20 minutes until it thickens while stirring occasionally.

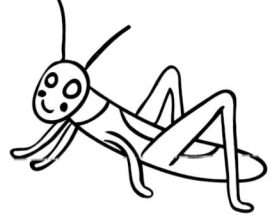

Veggie Tomato Sauce

This is my go-to recipe for all things tomato sauce. With extra veggies and the option to make it in the crockpot or on the stovetop, it's perfect for pasta, pizzas, school lunches, and dipping!

1 tablespoon (15 ml) olive oil

1 red bell pepper, diced

2 medium carrots, chopped

2 medium zucchini, chopped

1 rib celery, diced

1 small onion, diced

2 cloves garlic, minced

½ teaspoon salt

1 tablespoon (16 g) tomato paste

2 cans (28 ounces, or 800 g each) tomato purée

1 tablespoon (13 g) sugar

—

YIELD: Approximately 5 cups (1.2 kg)

Crockpot directions: Place all ingredients in a crockpot, and cook for 4 to 6 hours on low. Using an immersion blender, purée the sauce, so that no veggie chunks remain. Add water if needed for a lighter sauce consistency.

Stove-top directions: Heat the oil in a saucepan over medium heat. Add the bell pepper, carrots, zucchini, celery, onions, garlic, and salt. Sauté until the veggies are soft, about 5 minutes. Add the tomato paste, and cook for 1 minute more, stirring constantly.

Add the puréed tomatoes and sugar, reduce the heat to low, and simmer for 15 minutes. Remove from the heat, and purée with an immersion hand blender until smooth.

Return the sauce to the heat and simmer until thick, 10 to 20 minutes. For a thicker sauce, simmer for an additional 30 minutes.

LAURA'S TIP

Double this batch and freeze the sauce in individual servings.

KITCHEN NOTE

If you don't have an immersion blender, cook the sauce thoroughly and allow it to cool. Mix in your blender (in small batches) so that no chunks remain.

Homemade O's

Ditch the canned stuff. My homemade version packs a lot more nutrition and is super easy to make.

14 ounces (400 g) pastina, ABC-shape pasta, shells, or macaroni

5 cups (1.2 kg) Veggie Tomato Sauce (page 84)

1 cup (100 g) grated Parmesan cheese, optional

—
YIELD: 8 servings

Cook the pasta according to package directions. Mix the pasta and sauce, adding a little water if the sauce is too thick.

Serve in a small bowl and top with the cheese, if using.

For a school lunch: Warm up Homemade O's and place in a warmed thermos container.

KITCHEN NOTE

Divide the prepared recipe into individual portions in freezer ziplock bags. Freeze, thaw, and warm when a quick meal or lunch is needed.

Chicken Cordon Bleu Pasta

If you want to score major mom points, be sure to serve this hearty meal for dinner. Not only is this family-size pasta dish a real crowd pleaser, it also yields enough leftovers for a generous serving for lunch the next day.

12 ounces (340 g) penne pasta

2 cups (475 g) Homemade Alfredo Sauce (page 83)

1 chicken breast, cooked and diced

1 cup (150 g) diced cooked ham

6 bacon strips, cooked and chopped

1 tablespoon (12 g) creole seasoning

¼ cup (25 g) grated Parmesan cheese

¼ cup (30 g) shredded Monterey Jack cheese

—
YIELD: 8 servings

Cook the pasta according to package directions. Drain, place back in the pot and set aside.

Add the Alfredo sauce, cooked pasta, chicken, ham, bacon, and seasoning to the pot. Stir to combine everything, making sure all ingredients are thoroughly mixed.

Pour the pasta into a 13 × 9-inch (33 × 23 cm) baking dish. Top with the cheeses.

Preheat the oven to broil. Place the baking dish on the oven's middle rack. Broil for 3 to 5 minutes, or until the cheese bubbles and turns light brown.

For a school lunch: Place the warm pasta inside a preheated thermos.

Midweek Penne Bake

My family loves this pasta for dinner and anytime in their lunches. Personally, I love the fact that it's so easy to make, I can prepare it with a toddler on my hip! Most of it, anyway.

8 ounces (84 g) penne pasta

1 cup (250 g) part-skim ricotta cheese

2 cups (490 g) marinara sauce

1 cup (150 g) grated mozzarella cheese, divided

½ cup (50 g) grated Parmesan cheese, divided

—
YIELD: 4 servings

Cook the pasta according to package directions. Meanwhile, preheat the oven to 350°F (180°C).

In a large mixing bowl, combine the cooked pasta, ricotta, marinara sauce, half of the mozzarella cheese, and half of the Parmesan cheese. Stir to mix well.

Pour into a greased casserole dish, or individual ramekins, and sprinkle evenly with the remaining mozzarella and Parmesan. Bake for 15 to 20 minutes, until the cheese has melted and the sauce is bubbly.

For a school lunch: Reheat the pasta and warm a thermos. Place the pasta in the thermos container and pack inside the lunchbox.

Broccoroni

This lunch comes together in about five minutes. It's a great way to quickly put together last night's pasta and leftover broccoli to use.

½ cup (55 g) macaroni pasta, uncooked

½ cup (35 g) broccoli, finely chopped

1 tablespoon (14 g) butter

½ tablespoon (4 g) all-purpose flour

⅓ cup (80 ml) milk

¼ teaspoon salt

¼ teaspoon black pepper

1 tablespoon (8 g) Romano or Parmesan cheese, shredded

—
YIELD: 2 servings

Cook the pasta according to the package directions, and drain.

Meanwhile, steam the broccoli until tender-crisp, about 5 minutes, and drain.

In a large saucepan, melt the butter over medium heat and whisk in the flour until smooth. Cook for 1 to 2 minutes on medium-low heat, stirring constantly. When it begins to turn a light golden color, gradually whisk in the milk. Bring the mixture to a boil, and cook while stirring for 2 minutes, or until the sauce thickens. Season with the salt and pepper.

Remove from the heat, and stir in the cheese and broccoli. Toss with the pasta to coat.

For a school lunch: Preheat the thermos and pack warmed Broccoroni, adding a few spoonfuls of warm milk if needed.

Lentil Soup

My grandmother made lentil soup like no one else, and this recipe is my best attempt at replicating hers.

2 tablespoons (30 ml) olive oil

1 medium onion, finely chopped

½ cup (65 g) finely chopped carrots

½ cup (60 g) finely chopped celery

1 teaspoon kosher salt

1 pound (384 g) lentils, rinsed

1 can (15 ounces, or 425 g) petite diced tomatoes, drained

8 cups (2 L) vegetable broth

½ teaspoon ground cumin

½ teaspoon black pepper

2 bay leaves

—
YIELD: 8 servings

Place the olive oil into a 6-quart (5.7 L) Dutch oven, and set over medium heat. Once hot, add the onion, carrots, celery, and salt, and cook until the onions are translucent and the vegetables are tender, approximately 6 to 7 minutes.

Add the remaining ingredients, and stir to combine. Turn the heat to high, and bring to a boil. Reduce the heat to low, cover and cook at a low simmer until the lentils are tender, approximately 40 minutes. Remove the bay leaves.

Optional: For a creamier consistency, remove 1½ cups (355 ml) of lentil soup and purée in a blender. Pour it back in the pot and mix to combine.

For a school lunch: Pack in a preheated thermos.

Ginger Carrots

When my seventeen-month-old devoured these at my in-law's house, I knew we were onto something! Since then, they've become a staple inside his thermos lunches. I typically serve these over Bombay Rice (page 80) or grilled chicken.

1½ pounds (680 g) carrots, peeled and julienned

1 teaspoon apple cider vinegar

3 tablespoons (45 ml) water

1 teaspoon fresh ginger, grated

2 tablespoons (40 g) honey

1 teaspoon ground cinnamon

1 tablespoon (15 ml) olive oil

Salt and pepper

—
YIELD: 6 servings

Preheat the oven to 350°F (180°C). Place the carrots in a greased ovenproof casserole dish.

Whisk the vinegar, water, ginger, honey, and cinnamon, and stir the mixture into the carrots.

Drizzle with the oil, and add salt and pepper to taste. Cover the casserole, and bake for 40 minutes.

Dad's Easy Bean Soup

This recipe is the result of my husband's ingenuity. While I was away on a business trip, he realized he needed to come up with a quick lunch, but all that was available was beans, broth, and salsa. So he set out to make an easy soup to fill the kids' thermoses that has now become a family favorite.

1 teaspoon vegetable oil

2 cups (520 g) Homemade Salsa (page 114)

1 teaspoon ground cumin

2 cans (15 ounces, or 864 g) black beans, drained and rinsed

1 can (16 ounces, or 454 g) refried beans

2 cups (475 ml) chicken broth

½ cup (58 g) shredded Cheddar cheese

—
YIELD: 4 servings

Heat the oil in a saucepan over medium heat. Add the salsa and cumin, and cook for 3 to 5 minutes or until thickened. Add the black beans, refried beans, and broth; and simmer for 10 minutes.

When the soup is done, fill the thermos, and top with the cheese.

Red Beans and Rice >

In New Orleans, you'll find these to be a staple every Monday for lunch, even in school cafeterias. My quick and easy version is delicious and perfect for any thermos lunch.

1 tablespoon (15 ml) olive oil

1 medium onion, diced

2 ribs celery, diced

1 green or red bell pepper, diced

2 cloves garlic, minced

½ pound (220 g) smoked sausage, sliced

1 bay leaf

½ teaspoon dried thyme

½ teaspoon cayenne pepper (optional)

8 ounces (227 g) tomato sauce

¾ cup (175 ml) chicken stock

1 can (15 ounces, or 512 g) kidney beans, rinsed and drained

2 cups (330 g) cooked rice

—
YIELD: 4 to 6 lunch servings

In a large saucepan, heat the oil over medium heat. Sauté the onion, celery, and bell pepper until they are softened. Add the garlic and the sausage, and sauté for an additional 2 to 3 minutes.

Add the bay leaf, thyme, cayenne pepper, tomato sauce, chicken stock, and beans. Bring to a boil, and simmer for 10 to 15 minutes.

Remove the bay leaf, and serve the bean mixture over the rice.

Tomato Veggie Soup

This is the perfect tomato soup to serve with a grilled cheese or homemade cheese crackers.

1 tablespoon (15 ml) olive oil

1 red bell pepper, diced

2 medium carrots, diced

1 zucchini, diced

1 rib celery, diced

1 small onion, diced

2 cloves garlic, minced

1 tablespoon (15 g) tomato paste

3 cans (28 ounces, or 396 g each) crushed tomatoes or tomato purée, with juice

2 cups (470 ml) vegetable stock

—

YIELD: 6 to 8 servings

Heat the oil in a saucepan over medium heat. Add the bell pepper, carrots, zucchini, celery, onion, and garlic. Sauté until the veggies are soft, about 7 minutes.

Add the tomato paste, and cook for 1 minute more, stirring constantly. Add the tomatoes and vegetable stock, reduce the heat to low, and simmer for 15 minutes.

Remove from the heat, purée in a blender until smooth. Return the soup to the stove, and simmer until thick, 10 to 20 minutes. The longer you simmer this soup, the thicker and more flavorful it will become. You can simmer up to 2 hours. If the soup is too thick for your family, add additional vegetable stock.

White Bean Pumpkin Soup

All of the festive flavors of fall—in one delicious lunch!

1 medium onion, diced

2 cloves garlic, minced

¾ cup (100 g) diced carrots (about 4 carrots)

1 cup (226 g) pumpkin purée

1 can (15 ounces, or 425 g) white beans, drained and rinsed

6 cups (1.4 L) vegetable or chicken stock

1 teaspoon dried oregano

½ teaspoon black pepper

1 tablespoon (15 ml) olive oil

—

YIELD: 6 servings

Turn on a crockpot to a medium/low setting. Add all ingredients into your crockpot. Stir to combine. Cook for 4 hours.

You can leave the soup chunky or insert an immersion blender and purée it to a smooth texture.

For a school lunch: Warm the soup in the morning and place in a preheated thermos.

LAURA'S TIP

This recipe freezes very well. Along with some warm whole wheat rolls, this is a fantastic dinner recipe!

Homemade Ramen

In middle school, my cafeteria served a cup of ramen noodles for one dollar. Feeling nostalgic, I worked with my friend Alison to develop this wholesome version.

2 tablespoons (30 ml) extra-virgin olive oil

3 cloves garlic, minced

½ teaspoon ginger, grated (optional)

2 medium carrots, sliced

1 medium leek or 2 or 3 scallions (white part only), cleaned and sliced

4 cups (940 ml) vegetable broth

1 cup (235 ml) water

2 to 3 tablespoons (30 to 45 ml) soy sauce

1 cup (130 g) frozen peas

Kosher salt and pepper to taste

1 pound (435 g) whole wheat angel hair pasta

—
YIELD: 6 servings

In a large pot, over medium-high heat, warm the olive oil. Sauté the garlic and ginger, if using, until fragrant. Add the carrots and leek. Continue to sauté until the leeks are translucent.

Add the broth, water, and soy sauce. Bring to a boil, and reduce to a simmer for 5 minutes. Add in the peas, and continue to simmer until the peas are no longer frozen. Season with the salt and pepper.

Meanwhile, in a separate pot, bring water to a boil and add the pasta. Cook until al dente, and drain. The pasta remains separate from the soup to keep it from getting soggy during cooking and storage.

To serve, place a small serving of pasta in a soup bowl, and ladle soup over the pasta. Serve immediately.

For a school lunch: Pack in a preheated thermos.

Chicken Taco Soup

My friend Corey has this ability to make just about anything in a crockpot. When she shared this recipe with my family, and everyone devoured it, I knew I had to share it with you!

1 onion, chopped

1 can (15 ounces, or 435 g) chili or pinto beans, rinsed and drained

1 can (15 ounces, or 435 g) black beans, rinsed and drained

1½ cups (195 g) frozen corn

1 can (8 ounces, or 245 g) tomato sauce

2 cans (28 ounces, or 820 g) petite diced tomatoes

1½ cups (355 ml) chicken stock

4 tablespoons (48 g) Arriba! Seasoning (page 58)

1 pound (452 g) boneless, skinless chicken breasts

1 cup (110 g) shredded Cheddar cheese

1 cup (230 g) sour cream

—
YIELD: 6 servings

In a crockpot, combine the onion, beans, corn, tomato sauce, tomatoes, and stock. Mix well to combine all ingredients. Add seasoning and stir.

Place the uncooked chicken breasts into the liquid, pressing down until covered by the mixture. Cook on low for 7 hours. Remove the chicken from the crockpot onto a cutting board. Using two forks, shred the chicken and add it back into the pot.

To serve, top bowls with cheese and sour cream.

For a school lunch: Pack in a preheated thermos.

< Mexican Soup

With mild, robust flavors, this soup is perfect to fill the thermos on a cold day.

2 tablespoons (30 ml) extra-virgin olive oil

1 cup (130 g) carrots, coarsely diced

½ cup (75 g) green bell pepper, diced

½ cup (80 g) onion, diced

2 small zucchini, chopped

2 cloves garlic, minced

2 teaspoons (14 g) ground cumin

1 teaspoon dried oregano

1 teaspoon chili powder

1 can (14 ounces, or 396 g) petite diced tomatoes, drained

4 cups (940 ml) vegetable broth

1 can (14 ounces, or 400 g) black beans, drained and rinsed

1 cup (235 ml) water

½ cup (95 g) uncooked brown rice

Cilantro for garnish

—
YIELD: 6 servings

Heat the oil over medium heat in a large soup pot. Add in the carrots, pepper, onion, zucchini, and garlic. Sauté until just tender, and add in the cumin, oregano, and chili powder. Stir and cook for 1 minute until the spices are fragrant.

Pour in the tomatoes, broth, beans, and water. Cover and simmer for 20 minutes.

Stir in the rice and simmer for an additional 35 minutes. Garnish with cilantro to serve.

Tortellini Soup

After you try this soup, you'll never want to eat canned chicken noodle soup again.

2 tablespoons (30 ml) vegetable oil

½ cup (50 g) celery, chopped

½ cup (65 g) carrots, chopped

¼ cup (40 g) onion, chopped

1 clove garlic, minced

¼ teaspoon ground cumin

2 bay leaves

¼ teaspoon black pepper

8 cups (2 L) vegetable stock

10 ounces (283 g) cheese tortellini, uncooked

Freshly grated Parmesan cheese (optional)

—
YIELD: 8 servings

In a large pot, heat the oil over medium heat. Add the celery, carrots, onion, garlic, and spices. Cook stirring frequently, for about 7 minutes until the vegetables are tender.

Add the stock, and bring to a boil. Reduce the heat to low, and stir in the tortellini. Cover and simmer for 20 minutes.

Remove the bay leaves. Serve with sprinkled Parmesan, if using.

For a school lunch: Fill a preheated thermos with warmed soup. Serve with Parmesan Crostinis (page 104).

Southwest Quinoa

We weren't big fans of quinoa until we tried it this way. Make this hearty dish part of your lunchbox rotation.

FOR THE QUINOA:

2 cups (475 ml) water

1 cup (173 g) quinoa, rinsed and drained

¾ cup (195 g) jarred salsa

1 teaspoon chipotle chili powder

1 teaspoon ground cumin

¼ cup (4 g) finely chopped cilantro, plus additional for garnish

3 scallions, sliced thinly crossways

1 can (15 ounces, or 425 g) black beans, rinsed and drained

1 cup (130 g) frozen corn

2 medium tomatoes, chopped

FOR THE DRESSING:

½ cup (115 g) plain yogurt

1 tablespoon (15 ml) lime juice

1 teaspoon (6 g) salt

½ teaspoon (1 g) freshly ground pepper

1 teaspoon (3 g) garlic powder

Toppings:

1 avocado, diced

1 cup (115 g) shredded Cheddar cheese

—

YIELD: 4 servings

To make the quinoa: Bring the water to a boil, then stir in the quinoa, lower the heat, and reduce to a simmer. Cook for 10 minutes, and turn off the heat. Cover and let sit for 6 minutes—you'll know the quinoa is ready when you see the little white "tail" of the germ around the outside edge of each seed.

Once the quinoa is done, add the salsa, chili powder, and cumin, folding to combine well. Mix in cilantro, scallions, beans, corn, and tomatoes. Fold a few times until thoroughly combined.

To make the dressing: In a small bowl, whisk the yogurt, lime juice, salt, pepper, and garlic. Add the dressing, folding gently to combine.

Top with the avocado and cheese, and garnish with additional cilantro.

For a school lunch: Pack the leftovers in a container. This salad is great eaten cold or at room temperature as well.

CHAPTER FIVE

Extra Credit:
Staples, Drinks,
Treats, and More

*After helping thousands pack healthier lunches for their kids,
I've realized that a great lunch isn't just about the main
course. Of equal importance are all the extras that fill the
lunchbox. How could I write a homemade lunch cookbook
without sharing all of those special extras that help an
awesome lunch come together? This section includes my
pantry staples, my nontraditional sandwich bread recipes,
fun and nutritious smoothies, my go-to dips, and my kids'
favorite treats.Many of the parents in my community find
this section the tipping point of going fully homemade. This
section will be one of your most visited, guaranteed.*

Honey Wheat Biscuits

Wanting to find an alternative to pre-made canned dough, I finally created a recipe my entire family loves. Do not attempt to make this recipe with 100 percent whole wheat flour, or the biscuits will be very dense.

1 cup (125 g) all-purpose flour, plus more for dusting

1 cup (120 g) whole wheat flour

1½ tablespoons (7 g) baking powder

6 tablespoons (85 g) very cold unsalted butter

¼ teaspoon salt (omit if using salted butter)

¾ cup (175 ml) milk + additional for brushing

2 tablespoons (40 g) honey (optional)

—

YIELD: 6 large biscuits

Preheat the oven to 425°F (220°C).

In the bowl of your stand mixer, or a large bowl, add the flours and baking powder. Stir together.

Using a cheese grater, shred the butter and add into the bowl. For this reason, I always store a few sticks of butter in the freezer. Using your hands, mix the butter into the flour mixture until it's crumbly and evenly combined.

Form a well in the middle of the dry ingredients, and add the milk and honey, if using. Stir the flour mixture into the milk until a dough forms. Don't overmix.

Sprinkle some flour on your counter and knead the dough. Add additional flour until the dough is no longer sticky. Roll the dough with a rolling pin to about an inch (2.5 cm) thick. Cut the dough with a 2-inch (5 cm) biscuit cutter (or the top of a large glass). After the fourth biscuit, you might need to reshape and roll your dough for the final two biscuits.

Line your baking sheet with parchment paper or a silicone mat. Evenly space the six biscuits on the baking sheet. Brush the tops with milk, and bake for 13 to 15 minutes until a light golden brown.

KITCHEN NOTE

You must use a cheese grater for the butter. When I tested this recipe by cutting the butter into very small pieces with a knife, the dough did not rise well, and I had dense spots. Therefore, trust me, and take 20 seconds to grate the very cold butter.

Blueberry Bread

This bread is a staple in our home. The blueberries remind me of warm summer days all year round. Your kids will love it, and soon you'll be making two loaves at once!

1½ cups (218 g) blueberries, fresh or frozen

1½ cups + 1 tablespoon (196 g) all-purpose flour, divided

2 teaspoons (10 g) baking powder

½ teaspoon salt

1 cup (230 g) plain yogurt

1 cup (200 g) sugar

3 large eggs

2 teaspoons (4 g) lemon zest

1 teaspoon vanilla extract

½ cup (120 ml) coconut oil, in liquid form

—

YIELD: 1 loaf

Preheat the oven to 350°F (180°C). Grease a 9 × 5-inch (23 × 12.7 cm) loaf pan, dust with flour, and tap out the excess. Alternatively, you can line a loaf pan with parchment paper.

In a small bowl, mix the blueberries with 1 tablespoon (8 g) of the flour. Using your hands, toss them around until they are all evenly coated with flour. This helps prevent them from sinking to the bottom of the pan when baking.

In a medium bowl, whisk together the remaining flour, baking powder, and salt.

In a large bowl, or the bowl of your stand mixer, mix the yogurt, sugar, eggs, lemon zest, vanilla, and coconut oil on low speed until all items are thoroughly combined.

Slowly add the flour mix to the wet, making sure there are no lumps, but being careful that you don't overmix. Gently fold the blueberries into the batter. Pour the batter into the pan, and bake 50 to 55 minutes, or until a toothpick comes out clean.

Let the bread cool in the pan for 10 minutes, and then transfer to a wire rack to cool completely before removing from the pan.

Lemon Bread

Sweet and full of lemon flavor, this lemon bread is a household favorite after Sunday service.

FOR THE BREAD:

½ cup (112 g) butter

1 cup (200 g) sugar

2 large eggs

½ cup (120 ml) milk

1½ cups (188 g) all-purpose flour

1 teaspoon baking powder

½ teaspoon salt

1½ teaspoons lemon zest

FOR THE OPTIONAL GLAZE:

1 lemon, juiced

¼ cup (25 g) powdered sugar

—

YIELD: 1 loaf

Preheat the oven to 350°F (180°C). Grease and flour an 8 × 4-inch (20.3 × 10.2 cm) baking pan.

Cream the butter and sugar in a large bowl. Add the eggs, one at a time, until creamy. Add in the milk, and blend on low speed until combined.

In another bowl, sift the flour, baking powder, and salt. Add the lemon zest and mix. Combine the dry and wet ingredients to create a batter. Pour the batter into the prepared loaf pan. Bake for 50 to 55 minutes, until a toothpick inserted into the center comes out clean. Allow the loaf to cool for 5 minutes prior to transferring to a wire rack to finish cooling.

To make the glaze (optional): Combine the ingredients and spoon evenly over the top of the loaf.

Peanut Butter Bread

I created this bread for my son Alex, who is on the "slim side" and needs all the calories he can get. Luckily, he loves it. It's divine, rich, and nutritious. Perfect for breakfast, or as a sandwich bread alternative.

¾ cup (115 g) brown sugar, unpacked

½ cup (125 g) applesauce

½ cup (130 g) peanut butter

1 egg

1 cup (235 ml) milk

1 teaspoon (3 g) ground cinnamon

1 teaspoon (5 ml) vanilla extract

1¾ cups (218 g) all-purpose flour

1 teaspoon (5 g) baking soda

½ teaspoon salt

—

YIELD: 1 loaf

Preheat the oven to 350°F (180°C). Grease a rectangular bread loaf pan.

In your stand mixer, or a large bowl, combine the brown sugar, applesauce, peanut butter, egg, milk, cinnamon, and vanilla, and blend until a thick batter forms.

In a small bowl, sift the flour, baking soda, and salt. Slowly add the flour mixture into the wet ingredients.

Bake for 45 to 50 minutes, or until a toothpick inserted into the center comes out clean.

Banana Bread

I often use banana bread for sandwiches to give my picky son a little sandwich bread variety. This is a very basic, no-nuts recipe that my neighbor dropped off on a sticky note along with four overripe bananas. Was it a hint? Probably.

1¾ cup (218 g) all-purpose flour, sifted

1½ teaspoons baking soda

¼ teaspoon salt

½ cup (100 g) sugar

1 teaspoon vanilla extract

¼ cup (56 g) butter, softened

1 large egg

1 cup (225 g) mashed ripe bananas (1 or 2 bananas)

—
YIELD: 1 loaf

Preheat the oven to 350°F (180°C). Grease an 8 × 4-inch (20.3 × 10.2 cm) loaf pan.

Sift the flour, baking soda, and salt through a sifter or strainer into a large bowl.

In your stand mixer, or a large bowl, combine the sugar, vanilla, and butter, and beat at medium speed until smooth. Add the egg and beat until light in color with a fluffy texture. Add the bananas until thoroughly combined.

Slowly add the flour mixture to the banana mixture, and mix well until a thick batter is formed, but try to not overmix. Pour into the loaf pan, and bake for 40 to 50 minutes, or until a toothpick inserted into the center comes out clean. Cool completely before slicing.

LAURA'S TIP

You can use up to 1 cup (120 g) of whole wheat flour. Any more than that, and your banana bread will become a banana brick.

Pizza Dough

Friday night is usually our designated pizza night. This dough is my family's favorite. Lucky for busy parents everywhere, the dough freezes amazingly well. If you want to use whole wheat flour, I wouldn't go more than 50/50 whole wheat to white flour ratio on this pizza. Using additional whole wheat flour will make this a dense dough.

1 cup (235 ml) + 2 tablespoons (30 ml) warm water (120°F [49°C])

1 tablespoon (12 g) active dry yeast

1 tablespoon (20 g) honey

1 tablespoon (15 ml) olive oil

3 cups (375 g) all-purpose flour + additional for dusting

1 teaspoon salt

—

YIELD: 2 medium pizzas or 1 extra large

In a small bowl, combine the water, yeast, honey, and olive oil. Mix with a spoon, and let it sit for about 10 minutes for the yeast to activate. Once you see about 1 to 2 inches (2.5 to 5 cm) of froth, the yeast is done.

In the bowl of your stand mixer, or a large bowl, add the flour and salt. Mix it well. Slowly add the frothy water, and mix it (either with your hands or the paddle attachment) until you can form a dough ball.

Dust the countertop with flour. Place the dough on your countertop, and give it a thorough quick knead. You might need to add a little bit more flour to finish off the dough. The dough shouldn't be super-sticky or rock hard. Good pizza dough should have a "brand new play-dough" or softer consistency.

Rub the same bowl with olive oil, then place the dough inside, and give it a turn or two to coat. Cover it with a towel, and place it in a warm place to rise for about 1 to 1½ hours.

After the dough has risen, transfer it to a floured surface, and knead it a couple of times.

Oil a baking sheet and spread the dough on the sheet to make one large rectangular crust. Or divide the dough into two even portions, and make two smaller crusts. Bake on the sheet at 375°F (190°C) for about 25 minutes.

I like to use my pizza stone in a high-heat/short-cooking time setting. I bake this at 500°F (250°C) for about 10 to 12 minutes. You can, of course, use your stone at 375°F (190°C) for about 25 minutes.

Parmesan Crostinis

My grandmother used to make these plain, and I improved her wonderful recipe by simply adding a little Parmesan.

1 French baguette, sliced diagonally into ⅓-inch (1 cm) pieces

1 cup (100 g) grated Parmesan cheese (may need additional depending on the size of your baguette)

—
YIELD: 18 to 20 crostinis

Preheat the oven to 350°F (180°C).

Place the bread slices on baking sheets. Top the slices with the cheese, and place the baking sheet in the oven. Bake for 15 to 20 minutes, until the bread is crispy and the cheese is golden brown.

Cornbread Muffins >

These cornbread muffins are the perfect addition to the lunchbox! Whether you send them with a thermos full of hearty soup, or as a side with your favorite lunch, your kids will love them.

1 cup (140 g) cornmeal

1 cup (125 g) all-purpose flour

1 tablespoon (15 g) baking powder

½ teaspoon salt

1 cup (235 ml) milk

2 eggs

½ cup (115 g) butter, melted

½ cup (170 g) honey

—
YIELD: 12 muffins

Preheat the oven to 400°F (200°C).

In a large bowl, mix the cornmeal, flour, baking powder, and salt.

In another bowl, whisk together the milk, eggs, butter, and honey until the liquid is thoroughly combined. Gradually add the wet mixture into the dry ingredients, and stir until just mixed.

Place paper liners in a standard muffin tin. Divide the mixture into the papers, and bake for 15 minutes, until golden.

Easy Freezer Jam

During berry season, I purchase a lot of fresh berries on sale and freeze them for smoothies. Sometimes, I find a bag or two that have been in the back of my freezer a bit too long. But instead of tossing them out, I repurpose them into an easy-to-make jam.

6 cups (780 g) blackberries, raspberries, strawberries, or blueberries

1 lemon, juiced

1½ cups (300 g) sugar

—

YIELD: 3 cups (960 g)

Place all the ingredients into a 5-quart (4.7 L) pot, and bring it to a boil over medium to high heat. Stir occasionally, so the jam doesn't burn.

Bring the mixture to a boil, and simmer for about 10 minutes. Berry jam will begin to thicken. With a spoon, test for thickness, and when you are satisfied, turn off the heat.

Allow the hot jam to cool in the pot to room temperature. Divide the jam into 3 freezer zip bags.

Cinnamon Raisin Peanut Butter

We love cinnamon raisin everything at our house! And although this might sound a bit odd, this sweet cinnamon-flavored peanut butter tops the charts as one of our favorite spreads. Give it a try, and we're sure you'll love it too!

1 cup (260 g) peanut butter

1 teaspoon ground cinnamon

⅓ cup (48 g) raisins

—

YIELD: 1⅓ cups (346.6 g)

In a microwave-safe bowl, soften the peanut butter for about 15 seconds. Immediately add the cinnamon and mix well. Fold in the raisins. Store in a glass jar.

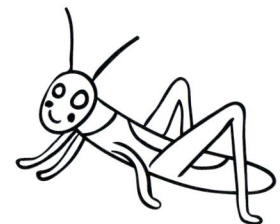

Easy Homemade Chocolate Spread

My kids love chocolate on everything. But when I looked at the store-bought kind and saw that the first ingredient listed was sugar, I knew I had to make my own. And we're so glad I did—this homemade version is creamy, nutty, and delicious!

2 cups (200 g) raw walnuts, toasted

1½ tablespoons (25 ml) vanilla extract

¼ cup (30 g) cocoa powder

¼ cup (60 ml) + 3 tablespoons (45 ml) pure maple syrup (may substitute honey)

¼ teaspoon salt

2 to 3 teaspoons (10 to 15 ml) melted coconut oil or vegetable oil

½ cup (120 ml) coconut milk

—
YIELD: 2½ cups (650 g)

In the bowl of a food processor, process the walnuts, stopping intermittently to scrape down the sides of bowl. Continue for 5 minutes until the walnuts have turned to thick, creamy butter.

Add in remaining ingredients, and blend for an additional 4 to 5 minutes, until smooth and creamy.

Refrigerate in an airtight container up to 3 weeks.

KITCHEN NOTE

Feel free to use whatever nut you like, or sunflower or pumpkin seeds.
Alternatively, you can use dairy milk, but this will cut shelf life to one week.

Caramel Peanut Butter

This caramel-flavored peanut butter is right on the borderline of being in the treat category. However, every lunchbox needs a little something sweet from time to time. Once you try this, you'll agree. The possibilities for enjoying this creamy, sweet spread are endless!

1 cup (175 g) caramel chips

1 tablespoon (15 ml) maple syrup (optional)

1 cup (260 g) peanut butter

—
YIELD: 1½ cups (390 g)

In a double boiler, melt the caramel chips, stirring continuously. Add the maple syrup, if using, as you stir. Once all caramel chips are melted, add the peanut butter, and continue to stir until everything is evenly combined.

Pour the peanut butter into two glass jars. Allow the jars to cool before closing.

< White Chocolate Peanut Butter

My daughter, the chocoholic, who won't eat peanut butter, actually loves this spread. Her imagination of what she will eat and dip into it runs wild every time I make a batch.

1 cup (175 g) white chocolate chips

1 tablespoon (15 ml) maple syrup (optional)

1 cup (260 g) peanut butter

—

YIELD: 1½ cups (390 g)

In a double boiler, melt the chocolate chips, stirring continuously. Add the maple syrup, if using, as you stir. Once all the chips are melted, add the peanut butter and continue to stir until everything is evenly combined.

Pour the peanut butter into two glass jars. Allow to cool before closing.

Flavored Cream Cheese

Many kids enjoy fruit-flavored cream cheese, but unfortunately the flavor often comes from artificial ingredients rather than real fruit. This recipe provides all the fun and flavor with far more nutritional value!

8 ounces (225 g) cream cheese, softened

½ cup (75 g) strawberries, room temperature

—

YIELD: 1¼ cups (281 g)

In a food processor or blender, combine the cream cheese and strawberries. Process until smooth and thoroughly mixed.

Store in an airtight container in the refrigerator for up to 10 days.

LAURA'S TIP

Use this same principle to create your own favorite flavor combinations, such as blueberry or raspberry flavored cream cheese.

Homemade Pesto

Packed with vitamin A, healthy fats, and calcium, this easy-to-make sauce brings a lot of flavor and nutrition to any lunch.

2 cups (80 g) fresh basil

¼ cup (25 g) grated Parmesan cheese

¼ cup (25 g) walnuts

1 clove garlic

½ teaspoon salt

¼ cup (59 ml) olive oil

—

YIELD: 1 cup (160 g)

Add all ingredients into a food processor, and purée until smooth.

Olive Salad

Full of flavor and so easy to make, this olive salad goes great with everything. Over pasta, in sandwiches, in panini's and wraps—the possibilities are endless.

½ cup (80 g) pitted green olives, chopped

½ cup (80 g) pitted kalamata olives, chopped

2 tablespoons (30 ml) olive oil

¼ teaspoon salt

—

YIELD: 1 cup (160 g)

In a large bowl, combine all ingredients. Mix well until the oil evenly coats the olives. Store in an airtight container for up to 10 days.

LAURA'S TIP

For a nut-free option, substitute sunflower or pumpkin seeds for walnuts.

Homemade Ranch Dressing Mix

The only way my daughter will eat raw veggies in her lunch is by dipping them in ranch dressing. Once I realized that I had all the ingredients to make my own, I was happy to not buy the store-bought packets again.

For the Mix:

¼ cup (5 g) fresh parsley, chopped

1½ tablespoons (5 g) dried dill

2 teaspoons (6 g) garlic powder

½ teaspoon black pepper

1 teaspoon dried chives

¼ teaspoon salt

—
YIELD: 4 packets (Each store-bought packet is approximately 1½ tablespoons [6 g])

In a small bowl, mix all ingredients together. If you want a fine powder like the seasoning packets, pour all ingredients in a coffee grinder and pulse a couple of times.

To make dressing: Mix 1½ tablespoons (6 g) of the mix with ⅓ cup (77 g) plain Greek yogurt and ⅓ cup (80 ml) milk.

To make dip: Mix 1½ tablespoons (6 g) of the mix with ½ cup (115 g) sour cream or plain Greek yogurt.

Greek Hummus

Nobody in my family makes hummus like Yanni. His smooth and creamy version is our favorite for spreading and dipping just about anything! Rich in protein and good for you omega-3s, it's the perfect companion in the lunchbox!

2 cans (14 ounces, or 398 g) chickpeas, drained and rinsed

3 tablespoons (45 ml) lemon juice

2 tablespoons (30 g) tahini

2 tablespoons (30 ml) olive oil

2 teaspoons (5 g) ground cumin

1 to 2 cloves garlic

1 to 1¼ cups (235 to 295 ml) water

Salt and pepper

—
YIELD: 2½ cups (284 g)

In a food processor or blender, combine the chickpeas, lemon juice, tahini, oil, cumin, and garlic, and mix for 1 minute.

Begin to thin with the water, adding it in slowly until you reach the thickness/consistency you desire. Season with the salt and pepper to taste. Refrigerate, in an airtight container, for up to 1 week.

For a school lunch: Pack along with fresh veggies for dipping.

Greek Yogurt Dip

Full of protein and bold flavor, this dip pairs perfectly with crunchy raw veggies.

½ cup (115 g) plain Greek yogurt

1 tablespoon (15 ml) lemon juice

½ tablespoon (7.5 ml) extra-virgin olive oil

1 clove garlic, minced

½ teaspoon dill, finely chopped

Salt and pepper

—
YIELD: 2 servings

In a bowl, mix all ingredients together. Season with the salt and pepper to taste. Refrigerate in an airtight container for up to 3 days.

White Bean Dip >

Who knew white beans could be this good!

1 can (15 ounces, or 425 g) white beans, drained and rinsed

1 clove garlic

¼ cup (15 g) parsley, loosely packed

2 tablespoons (30 ml) fresh lemon juice

3 tablespoons (45 ml) extra-virgin olive oil

½ teaspoon ground cumin

¼ teaspoon Arriba! Seasoning (page 58)

—
YIELD: 3 to 4 servings

Place all ingredients in the bowl of a food processor. Pulse until the mixture is coarsely chopped. Pulse a few more times until you achieve the puréed consistency you desire. Transfer to a small bowl.

For a school lunch: Pack along with fresh veggies for dipping.

Easy Guacamole

Making your own guacamole is so easy, you'll never buy store-bought again. Fresh is definitely better!

2 avocados, peeled, pitted, and meat removed

1 small shallot, minced

1 ripe tomato, diced small

1 lime, juiced

Salt and pepper

—

YIELD: 1¼ cups (281 g)

In a medium bowl, mash the avocados with a fork. Add the shallot, tomato, and lime juice. Combine well. Add salt and pepper to taste. Chill for half an hour before serving.

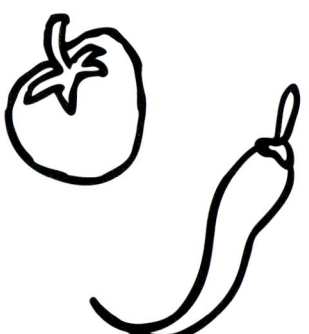

Homemade Salsa

So easy to make and far more delicious, you'll wonder why you've been buying the jarred stuff.

1½ cups (270 g) seeded tomatoes, chopped

⅓ cup (5 g) fresh cilantro, chopped

2 cloves garlic, minced

1 small shallot, finely chopped

½ jalapeño, finely chopped (less for a milder salsa)

2 tablespoons (30 ml) lime juice

Salt and pepper

—

YIELD: About 2 cups (520 g)

Mix all ingredients in a bowl until well combined. Season with the salt and pepper to taste. Refrigerate overnight for maximum flavor.

KITCHEN NOTE

For a thinner and not as chunky salsa, give all the ingredients a few pulses in the food processor.

Mango Madness Smoothie

Smoothies are a tasty way to enjoy nutritious fresh fruit. This tropical version is so refreshing—perfect for a warm day!

6 ounces (175 ml) pineapple juice

1 cup (175 g) mango chunks, fresh or frozen

1½ cups (355 ml) ice cubes

—

YIELD: 2 servings

Put pineapple juice, mango, and ice in a blender. Blend.

The Hulk (Green Smoothie)

It was very hard to convince my son that a green smoothie could taste good. If your child can get past the color, they'll love the flavor.

1 banana

1 cup (235 ml) pineapple juice

½ teaspoon vanilla extract

1½ cups (263 g) frozen mango chunks

2 large handfuls fresh baby spinach

—

YIELD: 2 servings

In a blender, combine all ingredients. Blend until smooth.

—

YIELD: 2 servings

LAURA'S TIP

Freeze smoothies in plastic freezer jars. Pull them out when you need them or throw them inside a lunch bag in the morning. They will act as an ice pack and be smoothie consistency by lunch!

Transform Your Smoothie Experience

I love smoothies in the morning, but I don't always have the time to put together a fresh smoothie while getting the kids dressed, fed, and out the door.

My friend, Michelle Castañeda, introduced me to making my own freezer packs, which are essentially just freezer bags filled with ready-to-blend combinations of fruits, or fruits and vegetables.

The concept has revolutionized my smoothie experience, making them convenient, while also completely reducing the amount of fresh produce we waste. For example: I used to purchase a big box of organic baby spinach at the grocery because it was cheaper than the small bag, but half the box would go to waste! Now, when I get home from the store, I put some in freezer bags right away (however much I know we won't be using for our meals), because Michelle taught me that freezing the spinach or other greens has no effect on the taste of the smoothie or on its nutritional value. The same thing goes for my overripe produce. It now goes into my freezer packs, so it's ready for smoothies at a moment's notice!

I've included some of my family's favorite smoothie recipes in this book, most of which can be prepped ahead of time in these packs. (And yes, I am one of those people who reuses her freezer ziplock bags!)

DIY Smoothie Freezer Packs

In a quart-size freezer bag, place dry (that is, nonliquid) smoothie ingredients. Squeeze all the air out of the bag and seal.

Label the bag with the amount of liquid and ice needed. Place the bag in the freezer to keep until ready to use. Servings will vary by recipe.

When you are ready to make smoothies, take the entire smoothie freezer pack and blend with the remaining liquid ingredients until completely smooth.

LAURA'S TIP

If you don't have a high powered blender, leave the smoothie pack on the counter for 5 to 10 minutes to thaw a bit so it's easier to blend.

Blueberry Lemonade Smoothie

This refreshing smoothie is perfect to send along with lunch on hot days.

1 cup (155 g) frozen blueberries

1 lemon, juiced

3 tablespoons (45 ml) maple syrup (or honey)

1½ cups (3.5 ml) lemonade

2 cups (475 ml) ice

—

YIELD: 2 servings

In a blender, combine the blueberries, lemon juice, maple syrup, and lemonade. Blend well.

Add ice and continue to blend. If it is too thick, add more lemonade or water.

Coconut Pie Smoothie

A guilt-free, sugar-free, creamy pleasure rich in coconut flavor!

3 bananas

¼ cup (65 g) cashew butter

1½ cups (354 ml) coconut milk

½ cup (40 g) coconut flakes

1 teaspoon vanilla extract

½ cup (120 ml) ice

—

YIELD: 4 servings

In a blender, combine the bananas, cashew butter, coconut milk, coconut flakes, and vanilla.

Blend well. Add ice and blend. If it's too thick, add more coconut milk or water.

< Homemade Chocolate Syrup

Real ingredients are what make this chocolate syrup okay in my book. Perfect for making chocolate milk or over your favorite ice cream sundaes. Your kids will never know you made this yourself, and they'll love it just as much.

½ cup (100 g) sugar

1 tablespoon (8 g) unsweetened cocoa powder

2½ teaspoons (7 g) cornstarch

½ cup (120 ml) water

1 teaspoon vanilla extract

—
YIELD: ⅔ cup (160 ml) syrup

In a small saucepan, combine the sugar, cocoa, cornstarch, and water. Over medium-high heat, bring to a boil, and reduce the heat. Stir continuously until thickened to a sauce consistency.

Remove from the heat. Add in the vanilla and stir. Pour into a glass jar and allow it to cool before storing.

To make chocolate milk: Use 1 to 2 spoonfuls of chocolate syrup per glass of milk.

Chocolate Chip Cookie Smoothie

Don't let the "cookie" in the name fool you. This healthy smoothie is both delicious and nutritious.

2 cups (460 g) vanilla yogurt

¼ cup (65 g) cashew butter (or peanut butter)

1½ cups (354 ml) milk

¼ cup (45 g) chocolate chips

1 cup (235 ml) ice

In a blender, combine the yogurt, cashew butter, milk, and chocolate chips. Blend well.

Add ice and continue to blend. If it's too thick, add more milk.

—
YIELD: 2 servings

Peaches and Cream Smoothie >

A tasty way of getting your kids' daily dose of vitamin C.

1 cup (250 g) frozen peaches

1 cup (235 ml) almond milk

2 tablespoons (30 ml) orange juice

½ cup (118 ml) ice

—

YIELD: 2 servings

In a blender, combine all ingredients and blend until smooth.

Vitamin C Cubes

These ice cubes flavor the water and add vitamin C. Perfect to help keep those cold bugs away!

One 16-ounce bag (454 g) frozen berries, softened

1½ cups (355 ml) orange juice

¼ cup (60 ml) lemon juice

—

YIELD: Approximately 4 cups (940 ml) cubes

Add all ingredients in a blender, and blend well. Pour and freeze in ice cube trays.

Place 2 or 3 cubes inside your water container.

Lunchbox Cheese Crackers

I receive a lot of emails with requests for healthier homemade versions of common packaged snacks to put inside lunchboxes. The cheese crackers one was no exception. This recipe is simple and easy to make, and it will leave you wondering what the extra ingredients in the box are for.

2 cups (240 g) grated white extra-sharp Cheddar cheese

¼ cup (55 g) butter, softened and cut into pieces

1 cup (125 g) flour + more for dusting

½ teaspoon salt

2 to 3 tablespoons (30 to 45 ml) milk

—

YIELD: 3 to 4 cups

Preheat the oven to 375°F (190°C).

Put everything except the milk in a food processor. Pulse the processor, 5 seconds at a time, about 5 or 6 times, until the dough is in coarse crumbs. Slowly add the milk and process until the dough gathers together into a ball.

Divide the dough into two balls. With a floured rolling pin, roll each dough ball out on a floured surface until it is about ⅛-inch thick. Cut the dough into 1-inch (2.5 cm) squares with a sharp knife or pizza cutter. You can put a bit of flour on the blade of the knife to keep it from sticking. Use a toothpick or skewer to poke a hole in the center of each cracker.

Place the crackers at least ¼ inch apart on parchment paper on a baking sheet.

Bake for 12 to 18 minutes until the edges are just starting to brown. They might puff up too. If you are baking two pans at the same time, swap/rotate the pans halfway through.

Slide the baking sheet off the pan onto a cooling rack, and let the crackers cool completely.

Eat or store in an airtight container or ziplock bag to eat within a few days.

Protein Cookie Bites

My great friend, Kelly Smith, developed these tasty cookie bites. Although we've never met in real life, I think of her each time I pack them in my son's lunch or after-school snack box.

½ cup (130 g) almond butter or peanut butter

¼ cup (85 g) + 1 tablespoon (20 g) raw honey or maple syrup

½ teaspoon vanilla extract

¼ cup (30 g), plus 1 tablespoon (8 g) coconut flour

3 tablespoons (21 g) ground flax seed

¼ teaspoon sea salt

¼ cup (44 g) mini chocolate chips

—
YIELD: 18 cookie bites

In a large bowl, mix together the almond butter, honey, and vanilla until creamy and well blended.

In a separate bowl, combine the flour, flaxseed, and salt. Add the dry ingredients to the wet, and mix well to combine. Use your hands to knead the dough. If the dough is too wet, add a bit more flour. If it's too dry and doesn't hold together well, knead in 1 teaspoon (5 ml) of water. Fold in the chips.

Scoop out spoon-size portions and roll into 1-inch (2.5 cm) balls, using your hands to create a bite-size treat. Store in the refrigerator.

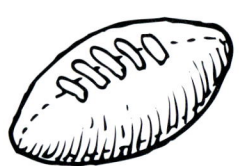

Chocolate Athlete Bars

If you have kids who participate in after-school activities, you know they need extra protein, calories, and nutrition to carry them through the day. Sadly, the best-tasting store-bought bars made with real ingredients are also expensive. Thanks to this recipe, we can ditch that habit and create our own no-bake bars with healthy ingredients—and save a lot of money too!

2 cups (160 g) quick oats

2¼ cups (259 g) blanched almond flour

½ cup (130 g) peanut butter (or any other nut butter)

⅓ cup (115 g) honey

¼ cup (30 g) cocoa powder

1 teaspoon vanilla extract

½ cup (120 ml) milk

—
YIELD: 10 bars

In a large bowl, combine the oats and almond flour. Set aside.

In a small saucepan, warm the peanut butter, honey, cocoa powder, vanilla, and milk. Slowly whisk the ingredients so that they melt and combine.

Pour over oat mixture and mix until a thick pasty mix has formed. I find that using your hands works really well to make sure all ingredients are thoroughly combined.

Line a 9 × 9-inch (23 × 23 cm) pan with parchment or waxed paper. Transfer the mix into the pan. Cover with plastic wrap and press down to spread uniformly. Make sure it's well packed down. Refrigerate at least 1 hour, preferably overnight.

Cut into bars or whatever shape you prefer. Store for up to 5 days in fridge or 1 month in the freezer.

KITCHEN NOTE

It's important to note that almond meal is not the same as blanched almond flour. Almond meal is ground almonds with the skins left intact, which results in a courser, denser flour with a heavier taste and texture. Blanched almond flour is finely ground almonds with their skins removed, which results in a lighter taste and texture.

< Ladybugs

This is one of the simplest snacks, yet kids absolutely love it. Maybe because it's so tasty and adorable!

2 tablespoons (32 g) peanut butter

1 apple, sliced

1 tablespoon (12 g) chocolate chips

—

YIELD: 1 serving

Spread the peanut butter onto the apple slices and decorate with chocolate chips.

Chocolate Chip Date Bars

My friend Alison, the photographer of this book, is an avid runner and mom to three active boys. She needs all the fuel and nutrition she can get from each bite. That's why she loves these delicious and nutritious bars! They not only provide her with a great source of energy, but also make a great snack bar for her boys as well.

1 cup (178 g) pitted dates

½ cup (75 g) peanuts

2 tablespoons (32 g) creamy peanut butter

⅓ cup (60 g) mini chocolate chips

—

YIELD: 6 bars

In a food processor, process the dates and peanuts until they begin to form a paste. Add in the peanut butter and continue to process until a dough begins to form. Next, add in the chips and pulse a few times to combine.

Line a 9 × 5-inch (23 × 12.7 cm) loaf pan with parchment paper or plastic wrap, and spoon in the mixture. Press firmly in the loaf pan, until about ¾-inch (2 cm) thick.

Refrigerate for 1 to 2 hours until firm. Lift up the parchment liner, remove from the loaf pan, and cut into 6 bars. Wrap individually and store in the refrigerator for up to a week.

Caramel Banilla Bites

When my friend Corey Valley told me about Banilla bites, I thought she was a genius! I've changed her recipe so that it uses my caramel peanut butter and boy, oh boy, are these delicious!

⅓ cup (87 g) Caramel Peanut Butter (page 107)

12 round vanilla wafers

1 banana, sliced into 6 thick pieces

Colored sprinkles, optional

—

YIELD: 6 servings

Spread a small amount of peanut butter onto each wafer. Place a slice of banana in the middle of 6 wafers, and top with remaining wafers.

Place sprinkles, if using, in a shallow bowl, and roll the cookies over the sprinkles a couple of times until the sides are covered.

Rainbow Fruit Cups >

This is the perfect way of making fruit portable, convenient, and slightly sweet without the unhealthy additives and sugars found in the packaged ones.

2 kiwis, peeled and cut into large chunks

1 cup (125 g) raspberries

1 cup (145 g) blueberries

1 tablespoon (20 g) maple syrup

—

YIELD: 4 servings

In a large bowl, combine the fruit and maple syrup. Toss well to evenly coat.

Distribute evenly among 4 small leak-proof containers.

< Frozen Yogurt Berries

Each sweet bite carries a little protein and vitamin C. It's the perfect afterschool snack!

6 ounces (145 g) fresh blueberries, washed

12 ounces (345 g) vanilla Greek yogurt

1 cup (145 g) fresh strawberries, washed

—

YIELD: 6 servings, or 3 cups

Line a baking sheet with parchment paper.

Using a toothpick, dip each blueberry into the yogurt and swirl until the blueberry is nicely coated with yogurt. Place on the baking sheet. Continue until all the blueberries are coated.

Dip the strawberries into the yogurt halfway up and lay on the baking sheet. Place the baking sheet into the freezer for at least an hour.

The strawberries should be consumed after an hour of freezing for the best flavor. Place any leftover strawberries in a ziplock bag and freeze for use in smoothies. The blueberries can be placed in a ziplock baggie and stored in the freezer. Take out what you need for snack time and enjoy!

No-Bake Brownie Bites

These bite-size treats are the perfect brain food! Loaded with antioxidants, protein, and vitamins, they pack a nutritional punch in every yummy bite.

½ cup (73 g) raisins

1 cup (235 ml) boiling water

⅓ cup (114 g) honey

2 teaspoons (30 ml) vanilla extract

1¾ cups (198 g) almond flour

3 tablespoons (41 g) unsweetened cocoa powder

⅓ cup (58 g) mini chocolate chips

—

YIELD: 12 brownie bites

Place the raisins in a small bowl, and pour the water over to cover. Allow the raisins to plump up for about 10 minutes, then drain and put the raisins in your food processor bowl.

Add the honey and vanilla to the bowl, and process until a thick paste forms. Add the flour and cocoa powder, and process until a dough has formed.

Transfer the dough into a bowl, fold in the chips, and refrigerate for 10 minutes. By doing this, the dough will be easier to shape. Once ready, use your hands to form and roll into bite-size balls. Refrigerate until ready to eat.

KITCHEN NOTE

Store brownie bites in the freezer for up to 3 months. For a lunchbox treat, stick them in the lunchbox frozen. They will thaw by lunchtime.

Strawberry Shortcake Kabobs

I love assembling a tray of these shortcake kabobs and keeping them in the fridge for play dates, an easy lunchbox treat, or lazy afternoon snack.

1 loaf Lemon Bread (page 100)

1 pound (510 g) fresh strawberries, whole or halved

½ cup (88 g) milk chocolate chips

½ cup (88 g) white chocolate chips

—

YIELD: 12 to 18 skewers

Slice the bread into ¾-inch (2 cm) thick slices. Cut into vertical strips, then into cubes.

Alternate skewering the bread cubes and strawberries through small wooden sticks. Once assembled, lay them flat on a baking sheet.

In the microwave, melt both milk chocolate and white chocolate chips in separate containers, making sure you stir every 15 seconds so that the chocolate doesn't burn.

Drizzle the melted white chocolate and milk chocolate over the kabobs. Allow the chocolate to cool, transfer the tray into the refrigerator, and store until ready to serve.

White Chocolate Peanut Butter Strawberry Crostinis >

When my friend Alison emailed me to tell me that her boys begged for these as their afternoon snack, I knew they were cookbook-worthy.

4 plain crostinis

2 tablespoons (32 g) White Chocolate Peanut Butter (page 109)

2 large strawberries, sliced

—

YIELD: 1 serving

Make plain crostinis from the Parmesan Crostinis recipe on page 104 by omitting Parmesan cheese.

Spread the peanut butter onto the crostinis. Top with the strawberry slices.

< White Chocolate Chip Cookies

Chocolate chip cookies are a lunchbox classic. This white chip version is a favorite with my kids, and I prefer them because they don't get their school clothes messy!

2¼ cups (282 g) all-purpose flour

1 teaspoon baking soda

1 teaspoon salt

1 cup (225 g) (2 sticks) butter, softened

¾ cup (200 g) granulated sugar

¾ cup (170 g) packed brown sugar

1 teaspoon vanilla extract

2 large eggs

2 cups (350 g) white chocolate chips

—

YIELD: 4 dozen cookies

Preheat the oven to 375°F (190°C).

In a small bowl, combine the flour, baking soda, and salt. In a large mixer bowl, beat the butter, granulated sugar, brown sugar, and vanilla until creamy. Add the eggs, one at a time, beating well after each addition.

Gradually beat in the flour mixture. Stir in the chips. Drop by rounded tablespoon onto ungreased baking sheets.

Bake for 9 to 11 minutes or until golden brown. Cool on baking sheets for 2 minutes; remove to wire racks to cool completely.

Halloween Loot Cookies

Swapping out chocolate chips for leftover chocolate Halloween candy will help you get through the loot a little quicker, and not in one sitting.

2¼ cups (282 g) all-purpose flour

1 teaspoon baking soda

1 teaspoon salt

1 cup (225 g) butter, softened

¾ cup (150 g) granulated sugar

¾ cup (170 g) packed brown sugar

1 teaspoon vanilla extract

2 large eggs

2 cups (350 g) chocolate Halloween candy, chopped

—

YIELD: 24 cookies

Preheat the oven to 375°F (190°C). Line two baking sheets with parchment paper.

Combine the flour, baking soda, and salt in a bowl. In a large mixer bowl, beat the butter, sugars, and vanilla until creamy. Add the eggs, one at a time, beating well after each addition. Gradually beat in the flour mixture. Fold in the candy.

Spoon golf ball–size dough balls onto lined baking sheets. Bake for 9 to 11 minutes or until golden brown. Cool on the baking sheets for 2 minutes; remove to wire racks to cool completely.

KITCHEN NOTE

Make extra batches of the cookie dough, and freeze single-portioned cookie dough balls for future baking.

Classroom Cupcakes

This recipe, adapted from Cooks Illustrated to make the process easier, became what I call a one-bowl wonder. It uses ingredients readily available in your pantry and comes together quicker than you can go to the store to purchase a box of cake mix.

FOR THE CUPCAKES:

1½ cups (188 g) all-purpose flour, sifted

1 cup (200 g) granulated sugar

1½ teaspoons baking powder

½ teaspoon salt

8 tablespoons (112 g) unsalted butter, room temperature

½ cup (115 g) Greek yogurt

2 large eggs, room temperature

1½ teaspoons vanilla extract

FOR THE FROSTING:

3 cups (300 g) powdered sugar

1 cup (448 g) butter, softened

1 teaspoon vanilla extract

1 to 2 tablespoons (15 to 30 ml) heavy cream

—

YIELD: 12 cupcakes

Adjust the oven rack to the middle position. Preheat the oven to 350° F (180°C). Line a standard cupcake pan with paper liners.

To make the cupcakes: In the bowl of your standing mixer, mix the flour, sugar, baking powder, and salt. Add the butter, yogurt, eggs, and vanilla, and beat at medium speed until smooth, about 30 seconds. Scrape down the sides of the bowl with a rubber spatula, and mix by hand until smooth and no flour pockets remain.

Divide the thick batter evenly among the cups (about two-thirds full) of the prepared tin. I like to use an ice cream scoop for this. Bake until the cupcake tops are pale gold and a toothpick inserted into the center comes out clean, about 22 minutes.

Remove from the oven; allow to cool for 5 minutes before removing the cupcakes from the tin and transferring to a wire rack. Cool the cupcakes to room temperature before frosting.

To make the frosting: In a large bowl, whisk the sugar and butter on low speed until well blended. Increase speed to medium, and beat for an additional 3 minutes.

Add the vanilla and cream, and beat on medium speed for 1 minute.

About the Author

Laura Fuentes is the founder and CEO of MOMables.com, where she helps thousands of parents every day make lunches their kids will love.

Laura is a speaker, recipe developer, and lover of all things mom. She partners with major real food brands to promote healthy school lunches, reduce childhood obesity, and teach healthy family eating.

In her personal blog, Laura writes about motherhood, good family food, managing deadlines, and keeping her cool, even when her kids super-glued her hair.

Above all, her most important job is caring for her family.

To find out more about Laura, visit www. LauraFuentes.com.

Index